There Were

in the

MorningStar Publications

A DIVISION OF MORNINGSTAR FELLOWSHIP CHURCH

375 Star Light Drive, Fort Mill, SC 29715

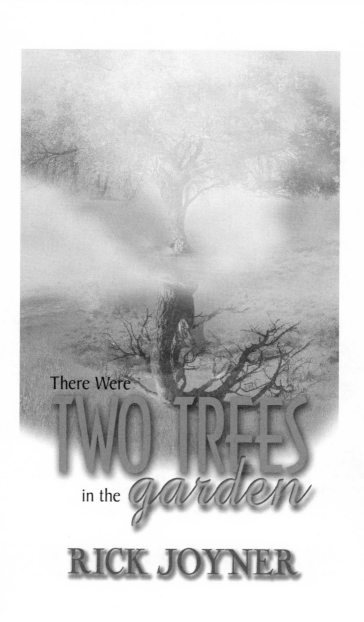

There Were

TWO TREES

in the *garden*

RICK JOYNER

There Were Two Trees in the Garden
by Rick Joyner
Copyright © 1986
New Edition, Mass Market, 2006

All rights reserved.

International Standard Book Number—1-929371-55-1

All Scripture quotations are taken from the New American Standard Version unless otherwise indicated, copyright (c) 1983 by Thomas Nelson, Inc.

TABLE OF CONTENTS

One...
The Two Trees...7

Two...
The Seed of Cain...17

Three...
The Sacrifice...31

Four...
The Root of Double-Mindedness...41

Five...
Babylon...55

Six...
The Antithesis of Babylon...65

Seven...
Abraham...73

Eight...
Looking for a City...89

Nine...
Jacob and Esau, Reuben and Joseph...99

Ten...
Pharaoh, Moses, and Spiritual Authority...111

Eleven...
The Fear of God vs. the Fear of Man...135

Twelve...
The Passover...145

Thirteen...
Taking the Lamb Into the House...161

Fourteen...
He Was Crucified by Us...167

Fifteen...
The Life Is in the Blood...179

Sixteen...
The Spirit Is Moving...193

Seventeen...
No Strangers May Eat of It...203

Eighteen...
The Victory...213

Chapter 1
THE TWO TREES

THERE WERE TWO TREES IN THE GARDEN OF EDEN THAT challenged the course of the entire human race—the Tree of the Knowledge of Good and Evil and the Tree of Life. Metaphorically, these same two "trees" continue to be the challenge that will determine the course of our lives. When we become Christians these challenges do not end—they may well increase, and many times we will have to choose between the fruit of these trees. Between them we find the focal point of the dichotomy between the kingdom of God and the domain of evil. Understanding this difference may be the most important understanding one could ever have.

When speaking of the two women who bore Abraham sons, Sarah and Hagar, Paul explained that they represented allegories, or symbolic representations, of biblical truths concerning the covenants of law and grace (see Galatians 4:21-26). In this same way the Tree of Knowledge and the Tree of Life also represent profound biblical truths that are crucial for us to understand if we are going to walk the path of life and avoid the snares of death.

In one way, they are symbolic of two spiritual lineages, or "family trees." The Bible, from Genesis to Revelation, follows the history of these two lineages. Understanding these lineages can help us to understand the most common errors which entangle the entire human race in the sin that leads to death, including those which have repeatedly been a stumbling block to the church. Understanding these lineages can also enable us to recognize and stay on the only path to true liberty and eternal life.

First, we must understand that Satan did not tempt Eve with the fruit of the Tree of Knowledge just because of the Lord's prohibition to not eat it. He tempted her with it because the source of his power was rooted in that tree. Furthermore, the Lord did not give this prohibition just to test Adam and Eve—He did it because He knew that the fruit of that tree was poison. When He instructed Adam not to eat from the Tree of Knowledge, He did not say "If you eat from that tree I'm going to kill you" but **"in the day that you eat from it you shall surely die" (Genesis 2:17)**. It was not *just* man's disobedience that brought death to the world, but the fruit from this tree.

What could be such a deadly fruit? The Tree of the Knowledge of Good and Evil metaphorically represented the law, which includes the Law given by God through Moses, as well as what we call "legalism." Legalism is adherence to humanly imposed laws which are implemented to try to make men righteous. Why did

God give the Law if its fruit was poison? It is for the same reason that He put the Tree of Knowledge in the Garden. As we will see, this was actually to free man so that he could have a special relationship to God.

However, this relationship would not come by eating from the tree, just as it cannot come through the Law. The Tree of Knowledge had to be put in the Garden because there could be no freedom to obey unless there was a freedom to disobey: There could be no true worship unless there was the freedom to not worship. We will examine this in more depth later, but this is why the apostle Paul declared, **"the power of sin is the law" (I Corinthians 15:56)**. This is because it is through the Law that we derive our knowledge of good and evil.

We may wonder how this knowledge brings death until we see the fruit. The knowledge of good and evil kills us by distracting us from the One who is the source of life: Jesus—the Tree of Life. The Tree of Knowledge causes us to focus our attention upon ourselves. The Law empowers sin, not just because it excites the *evil* in us, but because its remedy for resisting the evil is a form of *good* that is really self-righteousness instead of the righteousness provided by God through His Son, the Tree of Life. This knowledge derived through the Law will drive us either to corruption or self-righteousness, both of which lead us to death.

It is significant that the Tree of Knowledge is found in the center of the Garden (see Genesis 3:3). Self-centeredness is the chief malady with which it afflicts us. After Adam and Eve ate its fruit, their first response was self-inspection or self-centeredness. Before eating, they had not even noticed their nakedness—their attention was on the Lord and the purposes for which He had created them.

After eating, they were forced to measure themselves by the good and evil which they now understood. There is no easier way to keep us from the Tree of Life than to have us focus our attention upon ourselves. This is what the Law accomplishes. Because of this Paul called it **"the ministry of death"** and the **"ministry of condemnation" (II Corinthians 3:7, 9)**.

Again, when we define the Tree of Knowledge as the Law, we are not referring only to the Law of Moses. We often think of the Old Testament as the Law and the New Testament as grace, but this is not necessarily true. The Old Covenant is the letter; the New Covenant is the Spirit. If we read the New Testament with an Old Covenant heart, it will just be law to us. We will still have dead religion with righteousness that is based on compliance with written commandments instead of a living relationship with God.

The Lord said that He was going to send His Spirit to lead us into all truth. All truth is in Jesus. The Spirit was sent to testify of Jesus, to point us to the Tree with the fruit that gives life, not death (see John 16:13). The Bible is a most precious and wonderful gift from the Lord to His people, but it was not meant to take the place of the Lord Himself or the Spirit whom He sent. The Bible is a means, not an end. Knowing the Book of the Lord is not our primary goal, but rather to know the Lord of the Book. As wonderful a gift as the Bible is, it is not God. If it supplants the place of the Lord in our lives, it has actually become an idol.

Many fall into the idolatry of worshiping the things of God in place of God Himself. The reason for this can be found in the allegory of these two important trees which were in the Garden. We see in Genesis 2:9 that the Tree of Life was also in the center of the Garden. One of these trees will be the center of our lives and it is a choice that each of us must make.

There is a ditch on either side of the path of life. On one side there is legalism. On the other side is lawlessness. Both lead to death. If we tend to be reactionary, we will usually react to one of these ditches too much so that we end up in the one on the other side. God's answer to lawlessness is not legalism, but rather the cross. If we seek to be justified by the works of the Law, we are turning our backs on God's provision—the cross. If we turn from legalism without going to the cross, we will end up in lawlessness, one of the greatest evils to come upon the world in the last days.

Let us always keep in mind that the many errors and divisions within the body of Christ are not due to faults in the Bible, but our misuse of it. Some of the laws and principles wrested from the New Testament rival anything that the Pharisees did to the Old Testament! This has caused us to try to measure our spirituality by how well we conform to the letter. True spirituality is not found in adapting to a form, but by the forming of Jesus within us.

We must all choose between partaking of the Law and partaking of Christ; we cannot have both. This central truth is discussed at length in the book of Galatians and many other New Testament texts. Yet it seems that the application of this truth to our lives is frequently missed, and has repeatedly been the cause of many devastating conflicts between individual believers, churches, denominations, and movements.

The Letter Kills

It was for a good reason that the Lord instructed us to judge men by their fruit. A parrot can be taught to say and do the right things. Satan, likewise, often comes as **"an angel of light" (II Corinthians 11:14),** quoting Scripture just as he did in his temptation of Christ Jesus. His work will often impressively conform to the letter, but only Jesus can bring forth the fruit that is *LIFE*. **"The letter kills, but the Spirit gives life" (II Corinthians 3:6).** The serpent is still speaking from the midst of the Tree of Knowledge, compelling us to eat its fruit. We must learn to recognize this voice and reject it, regardless of how good the fruit on the tree looks.

One of the primary schemes of the devil is to turn the Bible into the Tree of Knowledge for us, instead of the Tree of Life. He is seeking to make it law to us rather than a revelation of Christ, in whom alone life is found. If we read the Scriptures by the Spirit, they will testify of Jesus and will come to life. **"You search the Scriptures, because you think that in them you have eternal life; and it is these that bear witness of Me" (John 5:39).**

The Spirit was sent to lead us to Him in the Scriptures and in all aspects of our lives. Reading the Scriptures without the Spirit brings only the knowledge of good and evil, or a form of legalism, which brings death through self-righteousness.

The cross gives life and keeps us on the path of life because it was His sacrifice, not ours, that is our justification. However, the devil will also try to get us to stumble in our devotion to the cross by having us base our righteousness on how we have taken up *our* crosses rather than on the atonement of the Son of God. This may sound too complicated, but it is actually easy and simple to distinguish such temptations—the temptation is to get us to focus the attention on ourselves rather than Christ. The fruit of the Tree of Knowledge always leads to self-centeredness. When we focus on Christ we are changed by beholding His glory, not ourselves.

Satan can counterfeit *form*, but he can never counterfeit the Spirit's *fruit*—which is Jesus, the Tree of Life. Man is able, to a certain degree for various self-centered and deceptive reasons, to change his outward behavior. Only the Spirit can change a man's heart. Therefore, the Lord looks upon the hearts of men, and in them He is looking for the heart of His Son. The Lord is not just trying to get us to do certain things and not do others; He is trying to conform us to the image of His Son, Jesus.

The Path of Light

Proverbs 4:18 says, **"But the path of the righteous is like the light of dawn, that shines brighter and brighter until the full day."** This is normal Christianity. When we come to the Lord a light should begin to shine on our path that becomes brighter and more clear until we are walking in the fullness of the light. However, this is not the testimony of many Christians, whose lives seem to be that of increasing confusion and darkness rather than light. Why is this?

There Were Two Trees in the Garden

This is a primary way that we should know we have somehow turned from the right path. In the Lord, the wrong path will never change into the right one. If we missed the right path, then the only way to get back on it is to go back to where we missed the turn. That is called "repentance."

The Lord's first act of creation was to bring forth light. The very next thing He did was separate the light from darkness. There can be no cohabitation between light and darkness. When a person is re-created and born again, the Lord immediately begins to separate the light from the darkness in his life. Almost inevitably, usually in our zeal for Him, we try to take over this work and perform it the only way we have ever known—through the knowledge of good and evil.

This struggle between law and grace and between flesh and Spirit is the source of the inner discord afflicting most Christians. It is also the single greatest point of conflict between the truth that sets men free and the lies of the enemy that are meant to oppress them, bringing forth death rather than life.

On the third day of creation, the Lord established a physical and spiritual law of critical importance. He ordered that trees would only bear fruit and produce seed after their own kind (see Genesis 1:11-12). The fruit of these two trees is to forever be separate and distinctive, as the Lord Jesus also testified: **"For there is no good tree which produces bad fruit; nor, on the other hand, a bad tree which produces good fruit. For each tree is known by its own fruit"** (**Luke 6:43-44**). Paul further stated: **"whatever a man sows, this he will also reap"** (**Galatians 6:7**).

The Two Trees

We cannot bring forth fruit that is life while we are partaking of the Tree of Knowledge. Likewise, if we are partaking of the Tree of Life, we will not bring forth the fruit of the Tree of Knowledge—death. A tree can only produce fruit after its own kind.

Trees are sometimes symbolic of family lineages, which is where we derived the term "family tree." So, these two trees in the Garden were, in a sense, a prophecy of the two lineages that would come forth in all of mankind. In order for Christ to come forth in man, His seed had to be sown in man. Likewise, in order for the "man of sin" to come forth in man, that seed also had to be sown in man. The fruit of a seed cannot be reaped unless it is first planted.

When Adam and Eve ate of the Tree of Knowledge, they were destined to perpetuate the fruit of that tree; consequently, death spread to all of their descendants. But God in His grace and mercy determined that He would redeem their mistake. He planted in man the seed which would again bring forth the Tree of Life—Jesus.

Through Him true life would be restored to man. His seed is a spiritual seed, sown by the Holy Spirit. No flesh could beget Him, but all flesh could receive Him. The Lord promised the transgressing woman that a seed would come forth from her that would crush the head of the serpent who had deceived her (see Genesis 3:15). In the first two sons born to the woman, we discern the seeds of each tree manifesting and starting to grow.

Chapter 2
THE SEED OF CAIN

A FTER THE TRANSGRESSION OF ADAM AND EVE, THE LORD prophesied the propagation of the two seeds—those who would embrace the nature of the serpent, and those who would be of the lineage which would bring forth Christ. Cain and Abel clearly reflected these two seeds, as well as the predicted enmity between them. Understanding this conflict can help us understand the basic conflict between the kingdom of God and the domain of evil.

Cain is a type of the fallen nature of man. As we are all descendants of the fallen man, this nature is in us all. Cain was the firstborn and is a type of the first man, Adam. Cain was of the earth, **"a tiller of the ground" (Genesis 4:2)**. This reflects a fundamental characteristic of those we will refer to as the seed of Cain—they are "earthly-minded." This includes all who have not been born again by the Spirit.

As the Lord Jesus testified, **"Unless one is born again, he cannot see the kingdom of God" (John 3:3)**.

Until we are born again by the Spirit, we can only see that which is earthly. Even if we come to know that there is a spiritual realm and spiritual power, it will still revolve around our own self-centeredness and an earthly, carnal perspective.

Just as the curse placed upon the serpent to crawl on his belly forces him to conform to the contour of the earth, so his seed is confined to the natural realm. **"But a natural man does not accept the things of the Spirit of God; for they are foolishness to him, and he cannot understand them, because they are spiritually appraised"** (I Corinthians 2:14).

This is our condition until the curse is removed in Christ. As we are born again by His Spirit, we begin to see and walk in heavenly places, and we become less and less subject to the contours of the natural realm. Jesus is no longer confined to this earthly realm, and if we come to abide in Him, we will be with Him where He is—above all rule, authority, and dominion on this earth, as Paul explained in Ephesians 2:4-7:

> **But God, being rich in mercy, because of His great love with which He loved us,**
>
> **even when we were dead in our transgressions, made us alive together with Christ (by grace you have been saved),**
>
> **and raised us up with Him, and seated us with Him in the heavenly places, in Christ Jesus,**
>
> **in order that in the ages to come He might show the surpassing riches of His grace in kindness toward us in Christ Jesus.**

We are called to be seated with Him above and to see everything from that position. This is the mature fruit of being born again. However, just as birth is not the end of life but the beginning, when we are born again we begin the process of growing into our new nature. Our minds have to be renewed or we have to think radically different than we did before. This is so different that, to paraphrase the way the apostle Paul said it, we should be more at home in the spiritual realm than the natural (see II Corinthians 5:6).

When we are born again, we begin our life as a part of the new creation which greatly transcends the old one. Before the Fall, the first-creation man could walk and have fellowship with God, but this is far short of what we have been given as the new creation. Now we do not just walk with God and have fellowship with Him—*He has come to live in us!* As the new creation, we have actually become temples of the Holy Spirit.

As awesome as it must have been for Mary to experience the seed of the Holy Spirit growing within her, as born-again believers we should have no less awe as we behold the Christ Himself living in our hearts by the Holy Spirit. Let's face it, if we had awakened this morning and seen Jesus physically manifested, standing next to our bed, do you think our day would have been a little different? Suppose He had gone along with us all day as our companion; would that have made a difference?

If so, we are still not walking as we should in the truth of our continual union with Christ. For if we see the spiritual reality that Christ is not only with us, but in us, we will have fellowship with Him *every day*, all day long. Our quest is not just to know who we are in Christ;

it is to know who He is in us. Walking in that reality is what it means to walk in truth.

The descendants of Cain, in their restricted vision, became worshipers of the creature and the creation instead of the Creator (see Romans 1:25). Cain is **"a tiller of the ground (Genesis 4:2),** which speaks of earthly-mindedness because that is all he can see. We can only worship that which we know. The culminating stages of self-worship bring forth the materialism and various humanistic dogmas that place man as the center of the universe. "Religious" man, whose devotion is to the church or to religious organizations rather than to Jesus Himself, is a "creature-worshiper." This attitude is also found among spiritualists who seek betterment, fulfillment, harmony, etc. by seeking unity with the creation instead of the Creator.

In the conclusion of God's written Word to man, the book of Revelation, we see the consummation of the two seeds that were sown in man. These are the "beast" and the glorified Christ. Though we can witness the development of these two seeds throughout the Scriptures, in Revelation we are given a glimpse of their ultimate state of maturation at the conclusion of this age. It is of utmost importance that we understand the development and final revelation of these two seeds if we are to have a significant part to play in the epic battle between them.

The Revelation was not given to John only to unfold a coming sequence of events. The primary purpose of the entire vision given to John was to be a **"revelation of Jesus Christ" (Revelation 1:1).** We must understand this to understand the vision properly. Although a sequence of events takes place in the vision, these are all given for the purpose of revealing Christ. Not only is this essential for understanding John's vision, it is essential for understanding the entirety of God's revelation to man. Jesus is the Revelation, as Paul so clearly revealed to the Ephesians:

He made known to us the mystery of His will, according to His kind intention which He purposed in Him

with a view to an administration suitable to the fulness of the times, that is, *the summing up of all things in Christ, things in the heavens and things upon the earth...* **(Ephesians 1:9-10** emphasis mine).

The ultimate purpose of God is that all things will be summed up in His Son. As my friend Mike Bickle once stated it, "If we do not keep our attention focused upon the ultimate purpose of God, we will continually be distracted by the lesser purposes of God." The key to understanding everything God is doing on the earth, and everything He is doing in our individual lives, is to understand that it is all for the purpose of bringing us and the whole creation into union with His Son.

Our goal is not to just see the Book of Revelation as either history or future events, but to see it in light of the unfolding purpose of God to reveal His Son. The apostle testified that these were **"things which must shortly take place" (Revelation 1:1)**. Events did immediately begin to take place, and continue to occur, which perfectly corroborate this prophecy. "History" truly is *"His*-story." As the Spirit opens our eyes, we see Him and His purposes even in what may appear to be the terrible confusion of man's history.

The Man of Sin

In John's vision, there is also a great deal about the antichrist, or the "man of sin." This man of sin is the personification of *the sin of man*. He is a manifestation of our basic nature until we are changed in Christ. He is the mature fruit of the Tree of Knowledge. The root and power of the man of sin is the serpent; the beast had to be fully revealed in human form because whatever is sown must also be reaped. In this beast we see ourselves without Christ. By this revelation of the gross darkness and sin that is our fallen nature, we begin to perceive the depth of the unfathomable grace and mercy of God and our profound need to be utterly reborn in Christ.

Revelation 13:16-17 teaches that the beast has a mark which he attempts to place upon us. In chapter 14, verses 9-10, we see that terrible wrath comes upon all who take the mark. Many people strive to understand the manner in which this beast will attempt to place his mark on them, so they will know what to refuse and will be free from the wrath foretold. Yet often those who are frantically trying to avoid the mark of the beast are actually partaking of the *spirit* of the beast every day!

Will we be free from the curse of the mark if we refuse to take a physical mark, but are of the very *nature* of the beast? Just as the seal (literally, "mark") that the Lord places upon His bondservants is not a physical mark visible to our natural eyes, the mark of the beast is probably far more subtle than we have been led to believe. Regardless of the form in which the mark comes or has come, those who have partaken of the nature of the beast, the spirit of the world, will not be able to resist the mark or anything else the beast has to offer. Our only deliverance from the wrath of God is to be found in Christ. Taking a mark is not the real sin. The sin is found in worshiping the beast. The mark is merely evidence of such worship.

John further explains: **"Here is wisdom. Let him who has understanding calculate the number of the beast, for the number is that of a man; and his number is six hundred and sixty-six" (Revelation 13:18).** The number 666 is not used arbitrarily. Because man was created on the sixth day, the number six is often used symbolically in the Scriptures as the number of *man*. This number is further identification of the spirit of the beast, which is the spirit of fallen man.

In verse 11, we see that this beast comes **"up out of the earth."** He is the culmination of the seed of Cain—the one who was **"a tiller of the ground,"** or earthly-minded. The beast is the embodiment of religion that originates in the mind of man. He comes up out of the earth in contrast to Christ, who comes down out of heaven. Jesus can only be brought forth by the Spirit of God. The New Jerusalem, typical of the true church, the bride of Christ, also comes down out of heaven, testifying of her heavenly origin. She is born of God, not man.

If we are trusting in our knowledge of good and evil to discern the beast, we will easily be deceived. The nature of the beast is rooted just as much in the "good" that is in man as it is in the evil. Satan comes as an **"angel of light" (II Corinthians 11:14),** or *messenger of truth,* because good has always been more deceptive than evil. It was not the evil nature of the Tree of Knowledge that deceived Eve; it was the good. The "good" of the Tree of Knowledge kills just as certainly as the evil.

There Were Two Trees in the Garden

The evil nature of man is being manifested in these last days with increasing intensity, but so is the "good" of man which is rooted in the same tree. Just as the evil is becoming more blatant, the good is becoming more subtle and deceptive. For example, what would the popularity of a leader be today if he were to promise safe streets, a healthy economy, an end to substance abuse and pornography, and the restoration of our national dignity and military strength—*and* delivered on all these promises?

Adolph Hitler promised all these things to a Germany crippled by depression and war. The nation was starving and on the verge of anarchy, with a currency that was utterly worthless. In just four years Hitler not only balanced the budget, but also paid off a national debt! He did this when their debt was a higher percentage of their gross national product than America's is today. He took one of the most economically and militarily weak nations on the earth at that time and made it one of the most powerful nations, both economically and militarily. In only four years, he took a nation struggling with more than 50 percent unemployment to 100 percent employment.

Not only did Hitler dramatically improve the German economy and military, he also removed corruption, pornography, and perversion from the streets, and instilled such a resolve and vision in the nation that even some church leaders began to wonder if it was the beginning of the Millennium. Such a dramatic transformation of a nation has never been witnessed before or since. It was so remarkable that even Winston Churchill said if Hitler had died in 1939, he would have been considered the greatest leader in world history.

The Seed of Cain

In the face of such "miracles," one can understand the deception of the masses and their adulation of this man. Yet few church leaders have been willing to acknowledge the tragic deception which also came upon most of the church in Germany. Milton Mayor, in *They Thought They Were Free* observed, "Fascism came as an angel of light and German Christians, both Protestant and Catholic, welcomed Hitler as a gift from God. Nazism was seen as redemptive of a decadent society and came almost as a Puritanism to a majority sick of perversions and license parading as liberty."

Hitler used the church in Germany as a springboard to power. The dean of Magdeburg Cathedral exulted in the Nazi flags displayed in his church, declaring, "Whoever reviles this symbol of ours is reviling our Germany. The swastika flags around the altar radiate hope—hope that the day is at last about to dawn." Pastor Siegfried Leffler stated, "In the pitch black night of church history Hitler became, as it were, the wonderful transparency for our time, the window of our age, through which light fell on the history of Christianity. Through him we were able to see the Savior in the history of the Germans." Pastor Julius Leutheuser actually taught that "Christ has come to us through Adolph Hitler."

The entire German church did not reach this level of deception, but much of it did. This profound delusion was challenged by the extraordinary stand for truth made by some German Christians, such as Dietrich Bonhoeffer. Bonhoeffer's life is one of the twentieth century's greatest examples of how a few who hold to the truth without compromise, standing against the most powerful political and military machines with nothing but spiritual power will ultimately prevail. What was said of the righteous Abel can now be said of Bonhoeffer, "Though he is dead, he still speaks." His life continues to challenge true believers to rise up and boldly stand against the darkness of their time.

It now seems clear that the German church's superficial understanding of redemption opened the door to this terrible deception. The good that is in man will never redeem him from the evil that is in him. It is still from the same tree, and its poison will always result in death. The system whose coming appeared so good to the German Christians shocked the civilized world with its evil deeds, but its nature had actually not changed. The good in man is just the other face of the evil in man. Satan is capable of using either good or evil as a tool to bring about his purposes.

There were only a handful of German Christians who discerned the deception from the beginning. The same satanic mask is being promulgated today. Our discernment must be more than distinguishing good from evil; we must know the Lord's voice and follow Him.

Milton Mayer added a significant insight into the events in Germany preceding the war: "I felt and still feel that it was not just German man that I met, but MAN. He happened to be in Germany under certain conditions. He might be here under certain conditions. He might, under certain conditions, be I." The truth is that the same beast is within us all. It is the Adamic nature that continually beckons us to eat of the Tree of the Knowledge of Good and Evil.

Just because one claims to be a Christian does not prove that he is one. Some of the worst deceivers in history have pretended to come in God's name. The Lord Himself warned, **"For many will come in My name, saying, 'I am the Christ,' and will mislead many'"** **(Matthew 24:5).** Some have interpreted this as saying that many would come claiming to *be* the Christ and would mislead many, but that is not what He said. He warned that many would come declaring that He, Jesus, was indeed the Christ and yet would be deceivers.

History testifies that this certainly has come to pass and is usually repeated in every generation. Compared to some of the despots and popes who ruled the Middle Ages, Hitler could seem almost benevolent. Some of the most abominable atrocities ever committed by man were done by those who claimed to be *the church* during the Middle Ages. We forget history too quickly, and Satan continues to come as an angel of light, deceiving us with the same tricks.

As Christians, we often gravitate toward and esteem most highly those who are the most conservative and moral. Jesus did not. And He was ultimately crucified by Israel's most moral and upstanding citizens—not by those thought to be its worst sinners. The Lord declared to the conservative and moral people of His day that the publicans and harlots would enter the kingdom of God before they would. Those who consider themselves "good citizens," "moral people," or even "religious" may be further from the kingdom than the lowest pervert. **"There is no one who does good, not even one"** **(Psalm 14:3).**

The sinners and the demon-possessed humbled themselves before the Lord, but the religious and upstanding citizens held Him in contempt as not being as righteous as they were. Who is the enemy? As I once heard a recently enlightened pastor remark, "We have met the enemy and *HE IS US!*"

Many "good" causes being championed in the world today actually serve as distractions for Christians because they draw our attention away from our true calling. In most cases there is no question that the issues are just and right, yet they only deal with the symptoms—they leave the disease untouched. Although homosexuality is a flagrant perversion, it is only a symptom of a much deeper problem. Abortion is one of the great horrors of our time, but it, too, is just a symptom. Even communism and fascism in their most cruel and oppressive forms are but symptoms of the disease that afflicts the soul of man.

For centuries the church has been offering the world band-aids for a deep, mortal wound. What man needs is more than just behavioral changes. Instead of flailing at the branches, we must put an ax to the root of the tree. We must be born again. Man's basic nature must change.

In every man and woman there is the potential for either Christ or the man of sin to be revealed. For this reason the message of repentance has to be preached. Still today, only repentance can prepare the way for Him. To repent means more than to have feelings of remorse because of sin or to walk down some aisle; it means to *turn away* from sin.

Sin is not just a few wrong things we have done, it is the nature of what we *are*, regardless of whether the guise is good or evil. In Christ, to repent means to renounce *all* that we are—not only our transgressions, but also that which we consider to be our righteousness. The apostle

Paul clearly articulated this in his letter to the church at Philippi.

> Beware of the dogs, beware of the evil workers, beware of the false circumcision;
>
> for we are the true circumcision, who worship in the Spirit of God and glory in Christ Jesus and put no confidence in the flesh,
>
> although I myself might have confidence even in the flesh. If anyone else has a mind to put confidence in the flesh, I far more:
>
> circumcised the eighth day, of the nation of Israel, of the tribe of Benjamin, a Hebrew of Hebrews; as to the Law, a Pharisee;
>
> as to zeal, a persecutor of the church; as to the righteousness which is in the Law, found blameless.
>
> But whatever things were gain to me, those things I have counted as loss for the sake of Christ.
>
> More than that, I count all things to be loss in view of the surpassing value of knowing Christ Jesus my Lord, for whom I have suffered the loss of all things, and count them but rubbish in order that I may gain Christ,
>
> and may be found in Him, not having a righteousness of my own derived from the Law, but that which is through faith in Christ, the righteousness which comes from God on the basis of faith (Philippians 3:2-9).

There Were Two Trees in the Garden

Paul's righteousness based on the Law brought him into direct conflict with the Truth. He was a persecutor of true worshipers, as is everyone who tries to live by the Law. Just as Cain could not tolerate Abel, those who seek to stand by their own righteousness find the presence of those who stand by faith in Jesus intolerable. The righteousness of God, based completely on the atonement of the cross, strips away façades and lays bare the pride of man which would seek to stand on its own righteousness. The cross is the greatest threat to man's self-centeredness.

Paul testified to the Philippians that to know Christ he had to give up *everything* he was. When he perceived the righteousness of Jesus, he counted everything that he had so valued in life as rubbish. This is an infallible testimony. Everything we have accomplished becomes less than worthless as we acknowledge who He is and what He has accomplished. As the Queen of Sheba was breathless before Solomon's splendor, we are far more so before Jesus. And that which is the greatest threat to our self-will, the cross, becomes a source of peace and freedom so profound that it challenges all human comprehension.

Chapter 3
THE SACRIFICE

THE SPIRITUAL ROOTS OF CAIN AND ABEL ARE CLEARLY discerned by the offerings they brought to the Lord. Cain brought an offering of grain, which in the Scriptures typifies our own works. After the Fall, the ground was cursed so that it would only produce through man's toil and sweat (see Genesis 3:17-19). The grain was the fruit of Cain's sweat. Cain thought that his works would be acceptable to the Lord as a sacrifice. Descendants of the seed of Cain still feel this way, and will try to base their relationship to God on their works or behavior rather than on the sacrifice of Christ.

All who have not had a revelation of the cross are continually trying to balance the good and evil within themselves. They erroneously believe that the good they have done will outweigh the evil, thus making them acceptable to God. Their defense comes in various forms: "I'm a decent fellow," "I never hurt anyone," "I go to church," "I give to missions," ad infinitum. Benevolence offered as compensation for evil is an affront to the cross of Jesus and will never be acceptable to the Father. **"All our righteous deeds are like a filthy garment…" (Isaiah 64:6).** Thus, Cain's offering of works had to be rejected by the Lord.

Abel, however, offered a sacrifice of blood, which was a type and prophecy of redemption through Jesus: **"Without shedding of blood there is no forgiveness" (Hebrews 9:22).** In contrast to Cain's offering, Abel's sacrifice was pleasing to the Lord. This caused the conflict between Cain and Abel and is the root source of the conflict between the two seeds which rages to this day. *Until the end, it will be the sacrifice that is the main point of conflict.*

The Lord's acceptance of Abel's offering so angered Cain that he slew his brother. The murderous nature of the seed of Cain is actually a defense mechanism rooted in insecurity. The self-righteousness of those seeking to be justified by their own works is very shaky, and deep inside they all know it. Because of this, they are easily threatened by anyone who would challenge their delusion.

We have a good illustration of this principle in Saul of Tarsus prior to his conversion. He claimed that according to the righteousness based on the Law, he was found blameless (see Philippians 3:6). When confronted by the truth that righteousness can only be found in Jesus, his very life's foundation was challenged. Enraged, he sought to destroy that which he accurately perceived to be the greatest threat to his own righteousness.

The cross of Jesus utterly destroys every self-righteous presumption. There is no greater intimidation to the knowledge of good and evil than the cross. The wrath generated in the seed of Cain that is directed at the cross and those who live by it, is merely a desperate attempt at self-preservation. Understanding the matter from both sides, Paul confidently says: **"all who desire to live godly** [righteous] **in Christ Jesus will be persecuted" (II Timothy 3:12).** Through the prophet Isaiah, God made an astonishing statement:

> **Who is blind but My servant, or so deaf as My messenger whom I send? Who is so blind as he that is at peace with Me, or so blind as the servant of the Lord? (Isaiah 42:19).**

In a discourse with the Jews, the Lord expounded upon this revelation:

> **Jesus said to them, "If you were blind, you would have no sin; but since you say, 'We see,' your sin remains" (John 9:41).**

Saul learned this on the road to Damascus. He had to be struck blind in the natural before he could see spiritually. So does everyone who comes to Jesus. If we think that we see, then our sinful nature still remains. Only by His blinding light can our sin be removed. Not until we have been blinded, until we acknowledge our inability to see, can we receive true vision. As James stated: **"But He gives a greater grace. Therefore it says, 'God is opposed to the proud, but gives grace to the humble" (James 4:6).**

Abel

The Scriptures do not disclose whether Abel resisted Cain in their conflict, but if he was true to the nature of Jesus, he did not. Neither are we to resist personal injustices if we are faithful to Him, as He gave us instruction:

"You have heard that it was said, 'An eye for an eye, and a tooth for a tooth.'

"But I say to you, do not resist him who is evil; but whoever slaps you on your right cheek, turn to him the other also.

"And if anyone wants to sue you, and take your shirt, let him have your coat also.

"And whoever shall force you to go one mile, go with him two.

"Give to him who asks of you, and do not turn away from him who wants to borrow from you.

"You have heard that it was said, 'You shall love your neighbor, and hate your enemy.'

"But I say to you, love your enemies, and pray for those who persecute you

"in order that you may be sons of your Father who is in heaven; for He causes His sun to rise on the evil and the good, and sends rain on the righteous and the unrighteous.

"For if you love those who love you, what reward have you? Do not even the tax-gatherers do the same?

"And if you greet your brothers only, what do you do more than others? Do not even the Gentiles do the same?

"Therefore you are to be perfect, as your heavenly Father is perfect" (Matthew 5:38-48).

The Lord did not give us this commandment just for our own spiritual discipline. He gave it to us because there is a power in nonresistance to evil that crushes the serpent's head. It tears evil out by the roots, out of our hearts, and the heart of our aggressor. This commandment was given to forbid us from doing that by which evil is multiplied and perpetuated. If we attack another, verbally or physically, evil is released. But if that evil is not able to affect its victim's patience, peace, or love, that which **"…is not provoked, does not take into account a wrong suffered…bears all things…endures all things" (I Corinthians 13:5-7)**, then the evil that was released is bound and defeated. Every blow that we are able to absorb without retaliation or resentment begins to consume the evil in the one who delivers it, as well as any that may be resident within us. **"But if your enemy is hungry, feed him, and if he is thirsty, give him a drink; for in so doing you will heap burning coals** [of conviction] **upon his head" (Romans 12:20).**

It is very hard for the natural man to understand this principle. To him it seems that this only gives license to the evil. But there is a much higher spiritual principle involved. Satan cannot cast out Satan; anger cannot cast out anger; neither can resentment cast out wrath. If we react to evil, we are only multiplying the very demon we are seeking to cast out. But **"love covers a multitude of sins" (I Peter 4:8).** As Jesus explained, **"If I cast out demons by the Spirit of God, then the kingdom of God has come upon you" (Matthew 12:28).** Only the Spirit of God can cast out Satan and transform us.

Jesus cast out Satan by allowing Satan to nail Him to the cross. To all the world, including His own disciples, it looked as if He were the One being cast out, not Satan. As paradoxical as it seems, the greatest injustice the world has ever known accomplished the greatest victory over evil. God's victories almost always seem like defeats to the natural man.

The Lord allowed Paul to persecute His church, causing much destruction for a time. To many of the persecuted, this was probably very hard to understand. But the Lord knew it would ultimately accomplish in the vessel He had chosen to carry His name to **"the Gentiles and kings and the sons of Israel" (Acts 9:15).** After Paul encountered Jesus on the road to Damascus, all the rage turned into humility and comprehension of the grace of God. The one who had been forgiven much would love much.

After nearly two thousand years, the voice of this apostle remains one of the most powerful voices in the world. The church lamented greatly over the death of Stephen, but had she been able to foresee the ultimate effect his death would have on this young "Pharisee of Pharisees" who watched Stephen's martyrdom, she would have rejoiced. **"Precious in the sight of the LORD is the death of His godly ones" (Psalm 116:15).**

Jesus explained the principle this way:

> **Truly, truly, I say to you, unless a grain of wheat falls into the earth and dies, it remains by itself alone; but if it dies, it bears much fruit (John 12:24).**

Though we may not see the fruit immediately, whenever we lay down our lives or suffer persecution for the Lord's sake, there is a triumph over evil and a glorious harvest from the seed that dies.

Forgiveness

Abel's blood cried out from the ground (see Genesis 4:10), a prophecy that the blood of Jesus would cry out from the earth with the greatest message creation would ever hear. Jesus looked down from the cross at His tormentors without wrath or retaliation, but with mercy. He prayed, **"Father forgive them; for they do not know what they are doing"** (Luke 23:34).

These were not idle words. He meant it! He is not waiting until He comes again to get even. He forgave them. He knew they did not understand what they were doing. They lived in a darkness that could not be penetrated without the power of the sacrifice He had come to make for them, which they were accomplishing by their own hands. He did not come to condemn the world; it was already condemned. He came to save it. He has commissioned us with that same purpose. If it is to be accomplished through us, we, too, must lay down our lives.

Turning the other cheek to a personal affront is never easy; it was not even easy for the Lord. Even the hope that we may be able to die to our self-will a little more will not give us the strength to endure. As the author of Hebrews declares, there is only one way for us to suffer injustice in the right spirit: by **"fixing our eyes on Jesus, the author and perfecter of faith, who for the joy set before Him endured the cross, despising the shame, and has sat down at the right hand of the throne of God. For** consider Him who endured such hostility by sinners against Himself, so that you may not grow weary and lose heart" (Hebrews 12:2-3).

When Stephen fixed his eyes on Jesus, even the stones that were to kill him could not hold his attention. When he saw Jesus, he was filled with the love of God as he, too, begged forgiveness for his persecutors (see Acts 7:54-60).

If we are to walk with Jesus, forgiveness is not optional; it is a requirement. **"For if you forgive men for their transgressions, your heavenly Father will also forgive you. But if you do not forgive men, then your Father will not forgive your transgressions"** (Matthew 6:14-15).

The ability to suffer personal injustice without retaliation or resentment is an infallible sign that a believer has come to abide in Christ. **"For if we have become united with Him in the likeness of His death, certainly we shall be also in the likeness of His resurrection"** (Romans 6:5). If we have truly been crucified with Christ, the greatest injustices will have no effect on us. If we have died with Christ, we are dead to the world. What could possibly affect a dead man? It is impossible for a dead man to retaliate. If we have died to the world, what can the world do to us?

Have this attitude in yourselves which was also in Christ Jesus, who, although He existed in the form of God, did not regard equality with God a thing to be grasped,

but emptied Himself, taking the form of a bond-servant, and being made in the likeness of men.

**And being found in appearance as a man,
He humbled Himself by becoming obedient to
the point of death, even death on a cross.**

**Therefore also God highly exalted Him,
and bestowed on Him the name which is above
every name (Philippians 2:5-9).**

If the Lord Jesus, the Creator and King of the universe, would allow Himself to be humiliated for the sake of those who humiliated Him, how much more should we lay aside our rights for the sake of those whom He purchased with His own blood? The exalted King of Glory became the most humble man, from His birth to His death for us. How much more should we be willing to lay aside any claim to honor or position for His sake?

Under the Old Covenant we were commanded to love our neighbors as ourselves. In Christ the calling is much higher. **"A new commandment I give to you, that you love one another, even as I have loved you"** (John 13:34). Jesus did not just love us as He loved Himself; He loved us *more* than He loved His own life. He has commanded us to love one another in this same manner.

God's wrath will be poured out on this earth, as it already has been in many ways. But we must understand His wrath. Although jealousy is both a work of the flesh and a work of Satan (see Galatians 5:20 and James 3:14-15), it is said many times in Scripture that God is a jealous God. Is the Lord subject to the flesh or to Satan? Of course not! The Lord's jealousy is not like man's jealousy. **"For My thoughts are not your thoughts, neither are your ways My ways, declares the LORD"** (Isaiah 55:8).

Man's jealousy is self-centered, but God's ways are higher than our ways. His jealousy is a pure jealousy, stimulated by His love for us. Neither is His wrath like man's wrath. **"God is love" (I John 4:8),** and even His wrath is motivated by that which is His nature: LOVE. We often interpret His ways from the perspective of our ways, but His ways are infinitely higher. Viewing Him from our own perspective instead of through the Spirit has often caused man to distort the Scriptures and the purposes of God.

The apostle Paul exhorted us to **"Behold then the kindness and severity of God" (Romans 11:22).** To our limited human minds, God's kindness and His severity seem to contradict one another. This has caused many to gravitate to one emphasis or the other. However, if seen in the Spirit, there is complete harmony in His kindness and severity. It is because of His love for us that He is severe.

Since His ways are higher than our ways, if we are to understand His ways we must be elevated so that we can see from His perspective. He cannot be understood correctly from the human perspective. To the world the cross is foolishness, but when the Lord opens our eyes, we see a glory that transcends human comprehension. It was for this reason that Paul prayed for the eyes of our hearts to be opened, not just our natural eyes (see Ephesians 1:18). We must be born of the Spirit to truly see.

Chapter 4
THE ROOT OF DOUBLE-MINDEDNESS

W E WOULD DO WELL TO UNDERSTAND CERTAIN characteristics that are becoming more prevalent in modern men and women. None of these characteristics are new, but their increase is significant. Like almost all human problems, their source can be traced to our tendency to eat from the Tree of the Knowledge of Good and Evil instead of the Tree of Life.

James wrote that the double-minded man is unstable in all his ways (see James 1:8). This double-mindedness creates instability and is one of the most subtle, profound afflictions of the human race. Its manifestation is increasing greatly in both frequency and degree. It may well be the major contributing factor to the deep darkness and time of trouble prophesied to come upon the world in the last days.

What is double-mindedness? To be double-minded is to have more than one mind or personality. A common modern term for this problem is schizophrenia (in the traditional definition, understanding that some modern schools have changed this definition). In fact, the Greek word used by James in this text is a root word from which we derive the English word schizophrenia. We tend to think of schizophrenia in its most extreme forms, those in which drastic personality changes occur. These are often demonic in nature. But there are degrees of double-mindedness found in all who have not been transformed from the carnal nature of fallen man by the renewing of their minds in Christ. If we tend to have one personality at home, another at the office or job, another at church, etc., it is a symptom of double-mindedness and a fruit of the Tree of Knowledge.

Those who try to live by the knowledge of good and evil will be double-minded to at least some degree. Men were not created to live with this knowledge, and trying to do so creates instability within us. We may think such changes in personality are normal, that we are just being flexible. Yet what is considered normal by the world's standards is not normal for the man God has re-created! There may be strong-willed people who can resist the changes in personality better than others, but given the right circumstances they, too, will bend and change. The only true stability that man can ever know is the Rock—Jesus.

Self-Centeredness

One of the most dominating fears afflicting fallen man is the fear of rejection. Contributing to this fear is the self-centeredness incurred by the knowledge of good and evil, as well as the fact that it is inherently "not good for man to be alone" (see Genesis 2:18). This was the first thing that the Lord said was not good, and it is a root of many human problems. The Lord created man to need Him, and us to need one another. This need was created in us to be fulfilled, but because of the Fall and the distortion of man's nature, this fear can become a very unholy drive.

This fear of rejection can compel us to become the person we believe will be accepted or recognized, which will vary to some degree with each new group or situation. With each change we make to comply with external circumstances, there is a subtle erosion of the consistency and stability of our personality. Soon we are confused as to who we really are and therefore can be controlled almost completely by external circumstances.

As stated previously, the first thing that God said was not good was for man to be alone. Sin brought a breech between man and his God, and also between himself and his fellow humans. Even when there were just two brothers on the earth one of them basically said, "This world isn't big enough for the both of us!" Yet, Cain's loneliness only increased after his sin, as it does after every transgression. This greater loneliness results in an even greater fear of rejection, which often causes even more rejection. It is an ever increasing and tightening death spiral that can only be broken by reconciliation with God, which will also begin our reconciliation with other people.

The Deep Darkness

The recent infusion of humanistic, philosophical, and psychological theories that drive men further from their Creator is resulting in an ever increasing erosion of consistency in personality. In human transactions, whether between individuals or in international foreign policy, the oscillations are becoming more and more pronounced. A good example is the sweeping changes in public opinion indicated by political polls, which can be astonishing in the way they swing to extremes.

Our tendency to easily abandon one position for another is a telltale sign that we are fast losing our grip on just what we really believe. Powerful forces are at work to undermine human stability. The future result will be an avalanche of debauchery which the Bible calls the greatest time of trouble the world has ever seen.

Because our first parents tasted of the forbidden fruit—and whatever is sown must be reaped—every individual born on this earth has the inner knowledge of good and evil. Even though this knowledge has, to a degree, helped to keep man from utter chaos after our separation from God, it is still the root of man's inner discord and depression. As the Lord explained to Cain: **"Why has your countenance fallen?** [or, "Why are you depressed?"] **If you do well, will not your countenance be lifted up? And if you do not do well, sin is crouching at the door; and its desire is for you, but you must master it"** (Genesis 4:6-7).

Because of his inner knowledge of good and evil, Cain had to live by it. The Law is in every man. When man does what he knows is right, he feels good. When he does not, there is discord, regardless of how earnestly he tries to rationalize his conflicts.

It is impossible for fallen man to wholly comply with the Law in his heart. Sigmund Freud realized that the primary cause of man's depression was guilt, just as any honest seeker of truth will find when searching for the root of man's problems. However, because he could not see past the Tree of Knowledge, he supposed that the remedy was to be found in the very fruit that was causing the problem. Instead of teaching that the relief from guilt and resulting depression was to be found in doing what is right, he began to attack what he considered unrealistic morals and standards.

This assault on morals and standards has continued with great subtlety and effectiveness. Many of the present trends toward lawlessness that are permeating the world today can be traced back to Freud's doctrines. Through them the door was cracked open to the deepest, darkest corruption of the human heart. As Margaret Thatcher, the Prime Minister of Great Britain, accurately discerned, "The veneer of civilization is very thin." Freudian theories escalated the stripping away of this thin veneer. This was accurately foreseen by the psalmist several thousand years before our time:

> **Why are the nations in an uproar, and the peoples devising a vain thing?**
>
> **The kings of the earth take their stand, and the rulers take counsel together against the LORD and against His Anointed:**
>
> **"Let us tear their fetters apart, and cast away their cords from us!" (Psalm 2:1-3).**

Freud correctly perceived that the Law is the source of man's depression. The reason is that no one can live up to its standards, and the resulting guilt brings depression. Paul articulated this in Romans 7:19: **"For the good that**

I wish, I do not do; but I practice the very evil that I do not wish." Paul concurred that the Law was good, but he was evil. He explained, **"For I know that nothing good dwells in me, that is, in my flesh; for the wishing is present in me, but the doing of the good is not"** **(Romans 7:18)**. This conflict caused Paul to seek help in the only true solution to the dilemma, the Lord Jesus Himself.

Freud, in contrast to Paul, turned to self-centered, human reasoning, the cause of all the death and evil this planet has ever known. Instead of seeking the Lord's provision for our deliverance from the Law, Freud tried to rid man of the Law by pretending it did not exist—a devastating and fatal mistake.

This reasoning is so devastating and futile because it could never be accomplished without completely removing man's conscience, which is as much a part of his created makeup as any physical organ. Without standards of right and wrong, we are reduced to a species lower than the beasts and much more dangerous. In fact, to the degree that the doctrines of Freud have been adopted, this is exactly what has been taking place—men have become even more cruel and heartless than any beast.

The psalmist rightly discerned that attacking God's Law would only bring about confusion among nations. Even with the overwhelming evidence of these terrible consequences, the philosophy of "removing the ancient boundaries" is in some form permeating every society of the world, and this is releasing the **"deep darkness"** prophesied to come upon the earth (see Isaiah 60:2).

The more we seek to ignore the Law, the more depressed and schizophrenic we will become, because the seed of the knowledge of good and evil is in us all and cannot be removed. The confusion now being released is the result of this great battle going on in the hearts of men.

The historian Will Durant observed that it is customs which keep men sane. As he put it: "Without grooves along which our minds can move with unconscious ease, we become perpetually hesitant and gripped with insecurity." Railroad tracks may restrict a train's freedom to move about, but without them the train would go nowhere. In the same way, man is not truly free to live in this world without the restrictions that God has placed upon him. The very constraints which confine man to his set course also set him free to be what he was created to be.

If a train tried to leave its tracks and take off across the countryside, it would quickly become mired and unable to function. Since man decided to jump his "tracks," he has become increasingly mired in instability. Those who are choosing their own course to "freedom" are becoming the most bound of all. The tracks of good and evil are frustrating to man, but they serve to keep man stable until he comes to Christ.

The Onslaught of Humanism

During the 1950s a great fear of communism began to permeate the West, especially the United States. Out of this era arose a child-rearing psychology which would supposedly produce character traits better able to resist tyranny. This philosophy glorified self-will and self-assertion. Psychologists, contrary to the wisdom of the Scriptures, encouraged a restraint of parental discipline. They believed that discipline would hinder the free expression and independent development of the child's character. This generation, projected to be uncompromising in their ideals, actually became the student rebels, communists, and anarchists of the late sixties and seventies. They became the very enemies their parents were trying to train them to resist! The parents of this generation reaped hatred and contempt instead of the moral purity and love for freedom they expected. Why?

Again the law of flesh and Spirit explains: **"For the one who sows to his own flesh shall from the flesh reap corruption" (Galatians 6:8).** Only by sowing to the Spirit can that which is Spirit be reaped. To feed self-will is to feed self-centeredness. Those who are self-centered are not capable of noble thoughts or deeds, for they are only concerned about their own needs and desires. These will actually be the most easily subverted by tyranny.

Having the guidelines of authority eroded within themselves, they will seek security in that which is the most authoritarian. Any authority that appears weak or indecisive will be despised and attacked. All a tyrant has to do is promise security and the gratification of their flesh, and he has won their allegiance.

Self-centered people are not capable of attaining the higher principles of love, duty, justice, mercy, or even freedom, though they may vigorously preach these things. They may attach themselves to causes, but the basic motivation of such attachment will be self-centered—rooted in rebellion, a desire for personal recognition, or the need to be identified with a strong social entity. The cause itself will be of secondary importance at best.

Attaching themselves to noble or dramatic causes is merely an attempt to compensate for their excesses. The "me generation" has now come of age. Laying aside personal ambition to become a true servant of the Lord Jesus has become almost incomprehensible, yet this is the only course of true freedom. Until He is the center of our lives, we cannot know true sanity or true freedom.

Man was created in the image of God and can only know his true identity when he is rightly related to God. Schizophrenia, or having multiple personalities, is perpetuated by a frustrated sense of identity. The schizophrenia of man is increasing as he moves farther from the One in whose image he was made. Conversely, as we draw closer to Him, we come to know who we really are.

As we draw closer to Him, we will become the most consistent, decisive, stable people the world has ever known. External situations and social pressures will no longer bend us and shape us. The standard of the One who lives within us will be the light by which we live.

Jesus is the same yesterday, today, and forever. He never changes! Neither will the world be able to change us when our minds have been so transformed that we see with His eyes, hear with His ears, and understand with His heart. The witness of the God who lives within us will become greater than all of the world's pressures. He is greater than the world! (see I John 4:4).

Those who truly know their God are the most confident, humble, and peaceful people on earth. As the Lord spoke through the prophet Isaiah: **"Behold, I am laying in Zion a stone, a tested stone, a costly cornerstone for the foundation, firmly placed. He who believes in it [Him] will not be disturbed"** (Isaiah 28:16).

Jesus is the Cornerstone of the creation. He is the only foundation for human life. When He is firmly placed in our lives, neither the world, nor all of the powers of evil, can disturb us. When we come to truly know our God—not just *about* Him—changes in our personality will come from within, no longer from without. His perfect love casts out all fear. In Him we no longer are moved by fear of rejection or fear of anything else. In Him we do not live by fear, but faith.

The apostle John clearly and profoundly stated the difference between the two seeds:

> **No one who is born of God practices sin, because His seed abides in him; and he cannot sin, because he is born of God.**
>
> **By this the children of God and the children of the devil are obvious: anyone who does not practice righteousness is not of God, nor the one who does not love his brother.**
>
> **For this is the message which you have heard from the beginning, that we should love one another; not as Cain, who was of the evil one, and slew his brother.**
>
> **And for what reason did he slay him? Because his deeds were evil, and his brother's were righteous.**
>
> **Do not marvel, brethren, if the world hates you.**
>
> **We know that we have passed out of death into life, because we love the brethren. He who does not love abides in death.**

Everyone who hates his brother is a murderer; and you know that no murderer has eternal life abiding in him.

We know love by this, that He laid down His life for us; and we ought to lay down our lives for the brethren.

But whoever has the world's goods, and beholds his brother in need and closes his heart against him, how does the love of God abide in Him?

Little children, let us not love with word or with tongue, but in deed and truth.

We shall know by this that we are of the truth, and shall assure our heart before Him (I John 3:9-19).

The distinguishing characteristics of those who are born of God are practicing righteousness and loving the brethren. This righteousness is not based on keeping the Law because **"by the works of the Law no flesh will be justified in His sight" (Romans 3:20)** and **"Christ is the end of the law for righteousness to everyone who believes" (Romans 10:4).** He did not make an end of the Law by doing away with it, *but by fulfilling it* (see Matthew 5:17). By this and the atonement which He made for our sins, He has become our righteousness. Our "practice of righteousness" is to abide in Him.

This faith is neither the act of a strong will, nor of intellectual assent and agreement with certain facts; it is a condition of the heart. **"For with the heart man believes, resulting in righteousness" (Romans 10:10).**

Just believing with our minds will not accomplish this. True faith is of the heart, not the mind, and can only be accomplished through the new birth. Only the Spirit can beget that which is Spirit. The carnal nature of man (Cain) is at war with the Spirit. Only by the birthing of Christ within us can there be harmony with God. The strongest act of human will cannot accomplish this, as the apostle points out in Romans 10:6-7:

> **But the righteousness based on faith speaks thus, "Do not say in your heart, 'Who will ascend into heaven?' (that is, to bring Christ down),**

> **"or 'Who will descend into the abyss?' (that is, to bring Christ up from the dead)."**

We cannot bring Christ down or raise Him up. Salvation is beyond human attainment. Only Jesus can keep the Law of God's righteousness. If we focus our attention on the Law, our sinful nature will consume us. If we focus our attention on Him, we will be changed into His image, the image we were originally created to bear. In Him there is no sin. To the degree that we abide in Him, there will be no sin in us.

When Jesus was asked by a scribe to name the great commandment, He answered: **"You shall love the Lord your God with all your heart, and with all your soul, and with all your mind. This is the great and foremost commandment. The second is like it, You shall love your neighbor as yourself. On these two commandments depend the whole Law and the Prophets"** (Matthew 22:37-40). If we could keep these two commandments, we would keep the whole Law. If we loved the Lord with all our hearts, we certainly would not commit idolatry; if we loved our neighbor, we would not murder him, envy what is his, commit adultery with his wife, etc.

The whole Law is fulfilled in these two commandments. Love is the fulfillment of the Law. Jesus replaced the negatives of the Law, the "do nots," with one simple positive: LOVE.

Which of us really loves the Lord with all our hearts, or even our brother as ourselves? **"The LORD has looked down from heaven upon the sons of men, to see if there are any who understand, who seek after God. They have all turned aside; together they have become corrupt; there is no one who does good, not even one" (Psalm 14:2-3).** We would not even seek the Lord if He did not draw us. Which one of us is not convicted by I Corinthians 13? Only by abiding in Him can we practice righteousness. Jesus is our Righteousness. Jesus is the Love of God that has been shed abroad in our hearts.

We are transformed as we behold the glory of the Lord (see II Corinthians 3:18). This is not accomplished by seeing Him and then looking back at ourselves comparatively (through the Tree of Knowledge). Our calling is not primarily to be imitators of Christ, but to have Christ *formed* within us. When we begin to truly see His glory, we are too consumed with the wonder of Him to be aware of or even interested in ourselves and what we may have attained. When the twenty-four elders in the book of Revelation saw the Lamb, they cast their crowns at His feet (see Revelation 4:10). Who could boast in His presence?

When we start trying to define our position in Christ, we begin to lose that position. *He is* the finished work of

God. *He is* the finished work of the church. We are growing up into Him. The issue is not what we are, but who He is. He is the Tree of Life. If we are partaking of Him, we will live forever.

Chapter 5
BABYLON

THE BUILDING OF THE TOWER OF BABEL IS ONE OF THE MORE clear revelations of the substance and motivation of the carnal nature of man. In one sentence, the men of Babel sum up that which is a primary motivation of the earthly-minded:

> Come, let us *build for ourselves* a city, and a tower whose top will reach into heaven, and *let us make for ourselves a name*; lest we be scattered abroad over the face of the whole earth (Genesis 11:4).

The Lord created us for His pleasure, for fellowship and service. The only true fulfillment we will ever know is found in serving Him, yet the fruit of the Tree of Knowledge has turned us almost completely inward. Now man's only intent is to serve himself, an endeavor inevitably resulting in great frustration and confusion.

As ludicrous as the attempt to build a tower to heaven may seem, men have never stopped trying to build it. In fact, the history of man looks like a long succession of unfinished towers—the ruins of man's attempt to make a name for himself, and unite around various projects. Grievously, Christians have seemed just as determined to build these towers to heaven. Regardless of how piously we attach the Lord's name to our works, everything motivated by selfish ambition will come to the same end as the original tower—confusion and scattering. James explained that selfish ambition is **"earthly, natural, demonic. For where jealousy and selfish ambition exist, there is disorder** [confusion] **and every evil thing"** (James 3:15-16).

The Root of Christian Disunity

Babel means "confusion." God looked down on the men of Babel and determined that the scattering of their languages was the best solution to their folly. He saw the same folly as He looked at what many believed to be the Christian church in the Middle Ages. Much of the visible church was another form of the original tower—an attempt by men to reach heaven by their own works. So the Lord scattered its languages, too. Now we have over 10,000 different "languages" or denominations.

Regardless of how good it may seem, every work that is an attempt to gather people around something other than the Lord Jesus Himself has its origin in the carnal nature of man. Regardless of whether it is a building project, evangelical outreach, or a great spiritual truth, an attempt to gather people around anything or anyone but the Lord Jesus Himself will ultimately result in confusion. Certainly there is nothing wrong with projects, outreaches, or seeking doctrinal truth, but if these become our focal point, eclipsing the Lord Jesus Himself, He will ultimately have to separate us from them for our own good.

It is possible to accurately understand all Christian doctrine and yet not be a Christian. Being a Christian is not just understanding certain doctrines and spiritual principles; it is having our life in Jesus. If the truth leads us to Jesus, it has accomplished its purpose. But if the truth itself becomes the focal point, it is just another form of the knowledge of good and evil. Its fruit will be death, regardless of how true it is. The information found at the Tree of Knowledge may no doubt be true and factual, but there is truth that kills and there is *The* Truth who gives life—and we must learn to distinguish between them.

Most denominations originated with a genuine move of the Spirit which imparted truth to the church. These truths were meant to lead the church closer to Jesus, and unquestionably this was accomplished for many. However, with each of these movements there have always been people who never saw beyond the truth itself. They began to build their towers around the truths, rather than seeing them as mere stepping stones to *The* Truth. These towers have now become many of the denominations that are scattered across the spiritual landscape of Christianity.

Babylon is not just a physical reality; Babylon is in the heart. There are many "non-denominational" churches that are as sectarian as any denominational church. Likewise, there are some denominational churches where Jesus is truly the Head, and these have little or no sectarian spirit. There are some who have truth without life, and there are others who have life in Jesus, though they may not have a correct understanding of all doctrine.

There Were Two Trees in the Garden

As Thomas á Kempis reflected in his classic work *Of the Imitation of Christ*, "I would rather feel contrition than know the definition thereof... What does it avail a man to be able to discourse profoundly concerning the Trinity if he is void of humility and thereby displeasing to the Trinity?"

Fleeing from physical Babylon is not just leaving a denomination or sect; it is the removal of all barriers which separate us from the Lord and our brothers so we might freely love and freely serve both. The apostle Paul exhorted, **"From now on we recognize no man** [or church?] **according to the flesh** [externals]" **(II Corinthians 5:16).** Those who are against denominations inevitably go on to build the next one. Our quest must transcend beyond simply being against the errors of the past. We must go on to see the glory of the Lord and the city which He is building.

Truth is important. There are certain basic truths that we must have in proper order if we are to remain on the path which leads to life. But believers through the ages have separated over many doctrines that are not in this category. Christians, disciples of Jesus whom He said would be recognized by their love, have demonstrated the uncanny ability to agree on 98 percent of their doctrines and yet separate from one another over the 2 percent on which they disagree. Required agreement on nonessentials is almost always rooted in insecurity more than a genuine love for the truth.

Insecurity among the leadership of the body of Christ has been the source of as much division within the church as any other single factor. The insecure are threatened by even the slightest deviation from their own beliefs and tend to greatly overreact to such deviations. Polarizations can cause bitterness, leading to irreconcilable differences over even extremely petty matters. This is a symptom of authority not rooted in Christ.

Overreacting to those who challenge our positions is evidence that we are in fact building for ourselves instead of building for the Lord. If we are rooted and abiding in Christ, we will not be intimidated by even the most severe challenges. The one who derives his authority from above understands the Lord's supreme authority and power and will not be overly concerned with the opposition of men.

True Unity

Nothing is impossible with God. It would be a small thing for Him to have us all believing the same way about everything. Presently, He has a good reason for not doing this. We must first understand that our unity is not based on having identical doctrines. Such unity is superficial at best. True unity can only be found in Jesus. To focus our attention on Him, and learn to love and cover one another, is far more important than doctrinal conformity. When the Lord becomes our focal point, we will see doctrines and all else from the same perspective—His!

When the Lamb came into their midst, even the twenty-four elders of the church cast their crowns at His feet! Who could presume glory or position in His presence? It is only because of the lack of His presence in the church that we are subject to the many divisions we now have. One of the most sobering Scriptures in the New Testament is Revelation 3:20, where we see Jesus standing outside and knocking at the door of His own church to see who will open to Him. That may be the ultimate spiritual challenge for every believer—hearing the Lord's knock above the clamor of the people and the pressures of those who grapple for position.

We are exhorted to "**examine everything carefully; hold fast to that which is good**" (I Thessalonians 5:21). We are foolish if we do not examine everything carefully by the Word and the Spirit. Nevertheless, we are just as foolish if we examine things in the wrong spirit. The exhortation is to hold fast to that which is good, not that which is bad. Examination is not for the purpose of looking for what is *wrong*—but what is right. When we seek truth with the intent of challenging the positions of others, we are seeking from such a wrong foundation that we will not be able to accurately perceive the truth.

Many Christians seem to have more faith in the devil's ability to deceive them than they do in the Holy Spirit's power to lead them into all truth. Again, this is a manifestation of our insecurity and has led to much division and misunderstanding in the body of Christ. There are times when challenge or confrontation is necessary to bring correction. The New Testament epistles are largely a result of the apostles and elders doing just that. Even so, the Lord's correction heals and restores. Our abrasiveness or judgmental spirit can make healing and restoration much more difficult for a person who is in error.

Paul exhorted, "**Brethren, even if a man is caught in any trespass, you who are spiritual, restore such a one in a spirit of gentleness; looking to yourself, lest you too be tempted**" (Galatians 6:1). There are many glaring examples of men who fell to the same sins they brazenly tried to expose in others. **"God resists the proud, but gives grace to the humble" (James 4:6 NKJV).**

None of us can stand except by God's grace. Whenever we attack or expose the sins or errors of others, having pride that *we* are not like that, we have almost guaranteed our own ultimate fall. This is why many "heresy hunters" become mean-spirited and usually end up doing more damage to the church through divisiveness than the "heresies" they were trying to confront.

Almost every great truth imparted to the church has been carried to extremes by those who first received it. As a result, other parts of the church often embrace the opposite extreme in overreaction. Frequently, the over-reactions have caused as much harm as the extremes to which the original doctrine may have been carried. Although those who are of either opposing position will consider it a compromise, the truth that leads to life is usually found somewhere between the two extremes.

Historically, the majority of the body of Christ has simply shied away from the controversial issues, wanting to avoid the confusion. This also is a mistake, for the wise will **"examine everything carefully"** and **"hold fast to that which is good" (I Thessalonians 5:21).** If we are living our lives more before men than before the Lord, we will easily be swayed by the pressure and confusion. If we are led by the Spirit, as all true sons of God are (see Romans 8:14), then He will faithfully lead us into all truth.

We must judge the fruit of a work before we devote ourselves to it, regardless of how "scriptural" it may seem. The Lord never said that we would know men or their works by how scriptural they are. Their true nature can only be known by their fruit. Is the fruit from the Tree of Life or the Tree of Knowledge? It does not matter how much "good" a work seems to accomplish—the Tree of Knowledge is rooted just as much in good as it is in evil. If the fruit is not Jesus, it is not life.

Most doctrinal errors are the result of an overemphasis on isolated Scriptures. That is why Paul exhorted Timothy to "**rightly [divide] the word of truth**" (**II Timothy 2:15 KJV**). Psalm 119:160 states, "**The *sum* of Thy word is truth.**" To rightly divide the Scriptures, we must see the complete Word of God. Many things in the written Word purposely seem contradictory. Because of this, we often gravitate toward one position or the other, overlooking what we do not understand, or worse, rationalizing our preference.

This tendency has led to polarizations over almost every Christian doctrine. We are often distracted from the River of Life by the little tributaries which feed it. Only when we are able to see the sum of all truth are we able to accurately understand any single part of it. *Jesus is the Sum of all spiritual truth.* All things will be summed up in Jesus (see Ephesians 1:10). When we lose our focus on God's ultimate purpose that all things are summed up in His Son, we become distracted by the *lesser* purposes of God, which we then carry to extremes. As we behold Him, all of the seemingly disconnected parts of God's plan and purpose come together in breathtaking harmony.

Walking in truth is not just understanding everything accurately; it is abiding in Him who is the Truth. Growing spiritually is not just to grow in knowledge but to "**grow up into him**" (**Ephesians 4:15 KJV**).

Deception is not just misunderstanding a doctrine; it is not being in His will. The body of Christ is not to be a conglomeration of many warring fragments; it is a living, functioning organism made up of different parts all contributing to the whole. The true body of Christ is not, and never was, divided. **"Since there is one bread, we who are many are one body; for we all partake of the one bread" (I Corinthians 10:17).**

The Pride of the Seed of Cain

The building of the Tower of Babel is a profound illustration of the pride of the seed of Cain. The people of Babel actually believed that they could reach heaven by their own efforts. **"Let us build...let us make" (Genesis 11:4).** This is an echo of the serpent's temptation of Eve— that she could become like God without God. Since the success of that temptation, Satan has been able to keep man devoted to this folly.

Man has fearfully bowed his knee to many idols, but he has always had one god—himself. The serpent tempted man to go his own way, and since that day man has been utterly determined to do just that. This inclination to independence brought death into the world and has been its perpetuating force. This is a reflection of Satan's own inclination. The prophet Isaiah articulated that the boast of the "king of Babylon," a personification of Satan:

> **"*I WILL* ascend to heaven; *I WILL* raise my throne above the stars of GOD, and *I WILL* sit on the mount of assembly in the recesses of the north.**

I WILL ascend above the heights of the clouds; *I WILL* make myself like the Most High" (Isaiah 14:13-14).

This attitude of being able to attain self-perfection is prevalent in every religion and philosophy in the world except one—*true* Christianity. The attitude of being a self-made person is so pervasive that many sincere and devoted Christians may not be aware of the extent to which this spirit rules their lives. Some of us have been so deceived that we not only think we can make ourselves what we should be, but others as well!

The irony is that the Lord *wants* us to ascend to heaven; He *wants* us to sit on the mount of the assembly; He *wants* us to be raised above the heights of the clouds; *and He wants us to be like Him* (to have His nature). But only He can accomplish this for us (which He has done through His Son). It has been a primary strategy of Satan through the ages to tempt man to grasp for himself what the Lord ultimately intends to give him anyway. The victory of Jesus over Satan was accomplished when He **"did not regard equality with God a thing to be grasped" (Philippians 2:6),** but humbled Himself instead, trusting the Father to exalt Him at the proper time.

Chapter 6
THE ANTITHESIS OF BABYLON

At Babel the Lord confused man's languages so people could no longer understand each other and continue building the tower of futility. On the Day of Pentecost, when the Lord first baptized men in His Holy Spirit, He provided a sign to the world that His church was to be the antithesis of the Tower of Babel. At Babel, man's languages were confused; at Pentecost, all men could understand a common language for the first time since Babel. By that common language they heard a testimony of the **"wonderful works of God" (Acts 2:11 NKJV),** in direct contrast to the futile works of man, typified by the tower.

Of course, the gift through which the crowd at Pentecost heard the testimony of God's works was the gift of tongues. It is not surprising that this gift would be the most controversial and divisive of the gifts of the Spirit. To the natural man, its purpose and practical use is very hard to understand. To the spiritual man, it is the language of God which penetrates all facades to touch the inner man. The language of the Spirit testifies of Jesus, the living Word [Greek, *logos*] of God, in whom all men will one day be found together in perfect unity. We will never be able to truly come into this unity until we give up our own languages to speak His.

When speaking of the common language, I am not talking about a language such as English, French, or German. We might all speak English and yet still not understand each other properly. The same word can mean radically different things to different people. For example, the word "family" may bring forth feelings of warmth, love, and good times to some, but memories of abuse, fears, and tragedy to others.

As someone once said, "We do not see the world as it is, but as we are." We can use the same words, even with the same accents, yet still not be able to understand each other until we see from the same perspective. The only way we will ever be able to see from the same perspective is to lay aside our own viewpoints —dying to them so we can view all things from the perspective of the Holy Spirit. The main reason the Holy Spirit is given to us is to change our view so that we might see with His eyes, hear with His ears, and understand with His heart. Only then will it be possible to come into true unity.

The Lord's judgment upon Babylon in scattering the languages was not done to condemn, but rather to preserve men until redemption could be accomplished for them. Only through Jesus can we truly be united. The Holy Spirit was given to reveal how desperately we need a redeemer and then to testify that the Redeemer is Jesus. No amount of ecumenical zeal or good intentions can bring men together without the Savior.

Our oneness can only be of Him and in Him. When He is truly lifted up He will draw all men to Himself. He is the only common denominator through whom there can be genuine communication and relationships among men and, even more importantly, between men and their Creator. Only through Him can we truly understand ourselves, others, and the Father.

Before the crucifixion the Lord prayed for His church **"that they may all be one; even as Thou, Father, art in Me, and I in Thee, that they also may be in Us; that the world may believe that Thou didst send Me" (John 17:21).** The religious institution that the world has tried to build is degenerating into increasing confusion, just as its predecessor at Babel. The church that the Lord is building will one day astonish the world with its unity. It will be a unity that transcends covenants and agreements; it will be a unity that could only come through a *union* with the One who holds all things together by the word of His power.

This unity will not come by seeking unity; it can only come by seeking Him. When unity comes, we may be completely oblivious to it because our attention will not be on ourselves but on Him. Although unity for its own sake can be a false god, if we are seeking Him, unity will come.

When Jesus was asked by the people, **"What shall we do, that we may work the works of God?"** His reply was to the point: **"This is the work of God, that you believe in Him whom He has sent" (John 6:28-29).** *Jesus is the finished work of God. He was the beginning of the work of God and He is the end, the Alpha and Omega.*

Understanding this, the apostle Paul had a single-minded purpose to his ministry: **"And we** proclaim Him, admonishing every man and teaching every man with all wisdom, that we may present every man complete in Christ. And for this purpose also I labor, striving according to His power, which mightily works within me" (Colossians 1:28-29). Jesus is the work of God. Everything that God is doing is found in Christ, just as the ultimate end of all things will be summed up in Him.

Jesus is called the "**Beginning of the creation of God**" (**Revelation 3:14**). In everything the Father brought forth by creation, He was first thinking of His Son. Jesus is everything the Father loves and esteems. He is the delight of the Father and the exact representation of His nature. The Father loves the Son above all, and the Son loves the Father above all. The Holy Spirit is the personification and power of this love. In everything that was created, the Father was looking for His Son. Today He is looking for His Son in us.

> **For by Him all things were created, both in the heavens and on earth, visible and invisible, whether thrones or dominions or rulers or authorities—***all things have been created by Him and for Him.***

> **And He is before all things, and** *in Him all things hold together*

> **He is also head of the body, the church; and He is the beginning, the first-born from the dead;** *so that He Himself might come to have first place in everything.*

> **For it was the Father's good pleasure for all the fulness to dwell in Him,**

And through Him to reconcile all things to Himself, having made peace through the blood of His cross; through Him, I say, whether things on earth or things in heaven (Colossians 1:16-20).

The labor of the apostles was not devoted primarily to persuading the churches to comply with certain doctrines, for their focus was on *Christ being formed* in the believers. Paul spoke of this to the Galatians: **"My children, with whom I am again in labor until *Christ is formed in you*" (Galatians 4:19).** This is the purpose of all true ministry—that Christ is formed. Jesus is the finished work. Our goal is not so much formation, but TRANS-FORMATION! The goal of all that we do is to become like Him and to do the works that He did.

He made known to us the mystery of His will, according to His kind intention which He purposed in Him

with a view to an administration suitable to the fulness of the times, that is *the summing up of all things in Christ*, things in the heavens and things upon the earth (Ephesians 1:9-10).

"That which is born of the flesh is flesh, and that which is born of the Spirit is spirit" (John 3:6). Only the Spirit of God can manifest Christ. Even the best human intentions can only bring forth that which is flesh. The best that man can offer is still rooted in the Tree of Knowledge. Because of this, Paul explained to the people of Athens: *"He* [God] *is not served by human hands"* **(Acts 17:25 NIV).** And Jesus testified: **"But an hour is coming, and now is, when the *true worshipers* shall worship the**

Father in spirit and truth; for such people the Father seeks to be His worshipers. God is spirit; and those who worship Him must worship in spirit and truth" (John 4:23-24). We will be worshipers to the degree that we are open to His Spirit to move through us.

True Spiritual Vision

Many who are born again and baptized in the Holy Spirit reflect no change in their approach to life. Though external behavior patterns may have changed, they continue to be cognizant primarily of the material realm. This may be due to the way they relate to Jesus. There is a tendency to continue relating to Him as "the *man* from Galilee." Jesus is no longer a man. He was and is fully Spirit. He took the *form* of a servant and became a man for a brief time, making a way for us to know Him by and through the Spirit.

The Scripture testifies that we are changed by the way we behold His glory (see II Corinthians 3:18). Beholding Him as a natural man does little to change us into the new creation He has called us to be. The Lord told Caiaphas: **"Hereafter** [or "from now on"] **you shall see the Son of Man sitting at the right hand of power, and coming on the clouds of heaven"** (**Matthew 26:64**). He was saying that after His crucifixion we would see Him in the power of His resurrection. When we begin to see Him in this light, we profoundly understand why **"he is not served by human hands"** (**Acts 17:25** NIV).

After His resurrection even His closest disciples had trouble recognizing Him. They were still more dependent on His physical appearance than His spiritual nature. Understanding this, He told them before

His crucifixion that it was expedient that He go away so His Spirit could be sent (see John 16:7). Men have historically had the tendency to know Him after the flesh rather than the Spirit. Jesus cannot be reduced to a natural-sense perception! We can never accurately perceive Him with just our natural eyes or natural minds. He can only be perceived through the Spirit. The Lord's challenge to Philip is still appropriate for the church today: **"Have I been so long with you, and yet you have not come to know Me, Philip?"** (John 14:9)

On the Mount of Transfiguration, we have a vivid example of an encounter between the glorified Christ and men who have not yet been transformed from the carnal nature of Cain. Matthew 17:1-8 reads:

> **...Jesus took with Him Peter and James and John his brother, and brought them up to a high mountain by themselves.**

> **And He was transfigured before them; and His face shone like the sun, and His garments became as white as light.**

> **And behold, Moses and Elijah appeared to them, talking with Him.**

> **And Peter answered and said to Jesus, "Lord, it is good for us to be here; if You wish, I will make three tabernacles here, one for You, and one for Moses, and one for Elijah.**

> **While he was still speaking, behold, a bright cloud overshadowed them; and behold, a voice out of the cloud, saying, "This is My beloved Son, with whom I am well pleased; listen to Him!"**

And when the disciples heard this, they fell on their faces and were much afraid.

And Jesus came to them and touched them and said, "Arise, and do not be afraid."

And lifting up their eyes, *they saw no one, except Jesus Himself alone.*

After observing Jesus' magnificent transfiguration, *"Peter answered!"* No one was even addressing Peter! And what came out of his mouth? **"It is good for us to be here…I WILL…"** Sound familiar? True, it was good for them to be there, but not for Peter's reasons. It was good for them to glimpse the glory of their Lord. It was good for them to heed the Father's rebuke: *"Listen to Him!"* They were not there to hear Moses (a type of the Law) or Elijah (a type of the church), but to hear Jesus! After they heard the command, it is recorded: **"Lifting up their eyes,** *they saw no one, except Jesus* **Himself alone."**

This was the purpose for which they had been brought to the mountain—their vision was to be focused on Him alone. We also must see Him transformed from "the Man of Galilee" into the glorified Son. We must hear in the depths of our beings the voice that exhorts us to forget about what *we* can build and to *"Listen to Him."*

Chapter 7
ABRAHAM

ABRAHAM OFFERS A PROFOUND CONTRAST TO THE MEN OF Babel. He was of a different spirit; his trust was not in himself but in the Lord. As the men of Babel strove to build for themselves an everlasting, earthly city, Abraham proved time after time his willingness to give up everything on earth to seek a heavenly city. He left his father's house and family in Ur of the Chaldees, drove out his firstborn son Ishmael, and even proved willing to sacrifice his promised son Isaac. Instead of striving to build a kingdom for himself, he continually released everything to the Lord, trusting Him to accomplish all that concerned him. Because of his faith, the Lord accomplished for Abraham all that the men of Babel had vainly sought—a name which would be esteemed for all generations and a city that would last forever.

Because natural men cannot really understand the things that are eternal, they often think if they can somehow become renowned among men they will not utterly perish. When we begin to perceive the Eternal One, to be remembered by men has little significance; to be known by the Lord is enough. As we perceive the glory of the Lord, all earthly cities and achievements begin to lose their attraction. Human claim to honor or position appears ludicrous. As we draw near to Him we lose interest in any city which man can build—the city which God has built will have all our attention.

Abraham was able to believe God because he was a man of spiritual vision; he was able to "look" at things which the natural eye cannot see. Being a spiritual man, he understood that **"the things which are seen are temporal, but the things which are not seen are eternal" (II Corinthians 4:18).** When the Lord opens the "eyes of our hearts" to the eternal realm, space and time cease to limit our vision; the future becomes as real as the present. Abraham was able to offer Isaac as a sacrifice because he had looked ahead to the sacrifice of Jesus, as the Lord Himself confirmed: **"Your father Abraham rejoiced to see My day; and he saw it, and was glad" (John 8:56).**

Abraham had prophetically foreseen the crucifixion and resurrection of Jesus, and he understood that his son Isaac was a type of the coming Messiah. Comprehending this, he made Isaac carry the wood for his own sacrifice, just as Jesus was to carry His own cross. Abraham knew that just as the Son of God was to be raised, so would his own son (see Hebrews 11:19).

True Faith

True faith is not a recipe that can be learned by rote. It is neither a feeling, nor an intellectual assessment and agreement with certain principles. True faith can only come with spiritual vision. The apostle explained that **"the eyes of** [our] **heart"** must be opened, for **"with the heart man believes" (Ephesians 1:18, Romans 10:10).** True faith is simply the recognition of the One in whom we believe. True faith is knowing Jesus. It is the ability to see Him in the power of His resurrection, as Abraham was able to do even before Jesus came. Faith is not just believing the words of the Lord, but believing the Word Himself. True faith is the ability to see eternity, an ability that delivers us from the cares and worries of this world which are passing away.

There are spiritual principles at work in the spiritual realm just as there are natural laws at work in the natural realm. These spiritual principles will work for anyone who uses them. In fact, even Satan's power is completely dependent upon God-ordained principles of spiritual power. Satan did not create the principles, God did. Satan merely bends them for his own purposes. Having faith in these principles, one can do mighty works completely apart from God. By this faith, many commercial faith healers and spiritualists perform their lying wonders. There are even sincere Christians who have wandered from the true faith to a faith reduced to spiritual principles—laws that can be learned and that indeed can work. The true faith of God, however, is based on a *relationship* with Him, not just the ability to comprehend and act upon a formula. Using spiritual formulas apart from God is actually a basis for witchcraft, which is counterfeit spiritual authority.

The difference between true and counterfeit faith is easily discerned by their fruit. True faith is directed toward God Himself; the other is merely faith in one's faith or reliance on principles and laws. True faith comes by seeing the Lord, and its fruit will be love and humility. The fruit of counterfeit faith will always be pride. It feeds the lusts of man and not his spirit.

Many of the doctrines that are called "faith" today are the result of dangerous grasping by those who are still earthly-minded. In these cases, the thrust of the teaching will place a great deal of emphasis on earthly blessing and attainment: **"For those who are according to the flesh set their minds on the things of the flesh, but those who are according to the Spirit, the things of the Spirit" (Romans 8:5).** Paul pointedly warned Timothy of the very thing that is today still making shipwreck of many Christians' spiritual lives:

> **But godliness actually is a means of great gain, when accompanied by contentment.**

> **For we have brought nothing into the world, so we cannot take anything out of it either.**

> **And if we have food and covering, with these we shall be content.**

> **But those who want to get rich fall into temptation and a snare and many foolish and harmful desires which plunge men into ruin and destruction.**

> **For the love of money is a root of all sorts of evil, and some by longing for it have wandered away from the faith, and pierced themselves with many a pang.**

But flee from these things, you man of God; and pursue righteousness, godliness, faith, love, perseverance and gentleness.

Fight the good fight of faith; take hold of the eternal life to which you were called (I Timothy 6:6-12).

To be rich or poor in the things of the world generally has nothing to do with our spirituality or our degree of faith. Some think it more spiritual to be poor and reject the resources the Lord wants to give to them because they do not believe it is God's will for them. Others just as foolishly devote themselves to material wealth at the expense of deviating from the path to the true eternal riches of the kingdom. Genuine faith is demonstrated by having peace in *whatever* circumstances the Lord has us in, as Paul testified:

…I have learned to be content in whatever circumstances I am.

I know how to get along with humble means, and I also know how to live in prosperity; in any and every circumstance I have learned the secret of being filled and going hungry, both of having abundance and suffering need (Philippians 4:11-12).

Was Paul lacking in faith when he went hungry? When he suffered need? By his own testimony, his contentment in those circumstances *was faith*. Nevertheless, just as we must learn contentment in times of need, we must also learn how to live in prosperity and keep a level head. If we cannot be responsible with the earth's riches, we certainly will not be capable of managing heavenly riches. But if we, like Paul, have perceived the spiritual riches in Christ, the world's riches will have little attraction for us.

This faith cannot be faked or conjured by a repetitious quoting of Scripture. It can only come from **"seeing Him who is unseen" (Hebrews 11:27)** as Moses did when he turned down all the riches of Egypt to follow Him.

The promises of God are not given so we can *do* and *have*, but so we can *be* (found in Him). That is why the promises of God are not made to us as individuals but to us in Christ, as the apostle explained: **"For as many as may be the promises of God, in Him they are yes" (II Corinthians 1:20).** This principle of receiving the benefit of a promise made to someone else is illustrated by Paul's words to the Galatians: **"Now the promises were spoken to Abraham and to his seed. He does not say, 'And to seeds,' as referring to many, but rather to one, 'And to your seed,'** *that is, Christ"* **(Galatians 3:16).**

Paul reiterated this in his letter to the Ephesians: **"I pray that the eyes of your heart may be enlightened, so that you may know what is the hope of** *His calling*, **what are the riches of the glory of** *His inheritance* **in the saints, and what is the surpassing greatness of** *His power* **toward us who believe. These are in accordance with the working of the strength of** *His might"* **(Ephesians 1:18-19).** Receiving the promises of God is dependent upon only one thing—receiving His Son and abiding in Him.

When Satan tempted Jesus in the wilderness, he tried to entice Him to claim the promises of God for selfish reasons. He is still using the same temptation today to cause Christians to stumble. The promises of God are glorious beyond comprehension, but none of them can be taken independently of Jesus. It is the Lord Himself who is our inheritance. The promises were given "in Him," for they are all given for His glory and His purposes. They were given in Him so all of our attention would be on Him—not ourselves. We do not perform great miracles by believing who *we* are in Christ, but by believing who He is in us. **"Truly, truly, I say to you, he who *believes in Me*, the works that I do shall he do also; and greater works than these shall he do; because I go to the Father"** (John 14:12).

The Great Separation

In the sixth chapter of John, a great separation takes place among the people who were following Jesus. In verse 2, we see a great multitude following Him *because* they were seeing the signs He was performing. Others were following Him because of the loaves He multiplied and fed to them (see verse 26). People have changed little—some still follow Jesus for miracles; others because of His provision for their needs. If a leader is intent on having great crowds follow his ministry, performing miracles, or preaching on God's provision, he will always bring out the multitudes. But Jesus knew that these motivations were superficial and would have to be changed. The line had to be drawn—the wheat and chaff separated. He challenged them: **"Do not work for the food which perishes, but for the food which endures to eternal life, which the Son of man shall give to you, for on Him the Father, even God, has set His seal"** (verse 27).

There Were Two Trees in the Garden

The crowd did not understand what Jesus was saying: **"They said therefore to Him, 'What shall we do, that we may work the works of God?'"** (verse 28). The Lord again tried to correct their motives: **"This is the work of God, that you believe in Him whom He has sent"** (verse 29). The multitudes' reply to this was to ask for a sign and for manna from heaven. The Lord answered that He *was* the Bread from heaven, and unless they ate His flesh and drank His blood, they would not have life. In one of the saddest testimonies of typical human motivation, John recorded: **"As a result of this many of *His disciples* withdrew, and were not walking with Him any more"** (verse 66).

When it was narrowed down to those who were following Him for who He was and not for what He could do, there were not many left. Those who withdrew were not just stragglers picked up by the excitement of the crowd—they were *disciples*. If the Lord were to make this same challenge today, how many would be left? Just as Peter supposed he would never deny Him, it is hard for us to believe that we would ever leave Him. But we are no different. When that challenge comes (and it will), how many will be left from the great multitude who now call themselves disciples? Will *we* be left?

At this point the ministry of Jesus dramatically changed. Until then He had devoted most of His attention to the multitudes; after this, most of His efforts were directed to the twelve disciples who remained with Him. Before this incident He had performed miracles so the people would believe in Him; from this point on, He only performed miracles for those who already believed in Him.

The Lord desires to bless His people, just as any loving father does his children. However, when we desire the blessings and gifts more than we desire Him, serious problems result. Self-centeredness is a poison that is killing us. When we receive His blessings in a way that perpetuates our egocentricity, in His mercy He often stops the blessings. The entire history of ancient Israel is a continuous cycle of deliverance, blessing, complacency, idolatry, bondage, oppression, humility, and seeking the Lord—then the cycle begins anew. They never did get the message. Will we?

The Lord calls the church to be His bride. How would any husband feel if he found out that his wife only married him for his wealth and that she would leave him if the expensive gifts stopped? Where would the joy be if the only time his wife communicated with him was when she wanted something? It would be a lifeless marriage. Is there life in our relationship with the Lord?

If the Lord had more of our attention than the blessings, we would no doubt be walking in more blessing. The promise is that if we seek *first* His kingdom, then everything else will be added to us (see Matthew 6:33). Of course He wants us to appreciate our inheritance, but compared to Him, all the treasures are insignificant! When we begin to really see Him, we will cast our crowns at His feet.

Faith and Patience

Hebrews 6:12 exhorts us to be **"imitators of those who through faith *and patience* inherit the promises."** While faith has been a very popular subject among Christians in the last few decades, the other necessary ingredient, *patience*, is usually overlooked. Have you not wondered why we have this huge "Faith Movement," but there is no such thing as a "Patience Movement?" Doesn't this verse declare that both are needed to inherit the promises? This oversight has sometimes been tragic.

True faith cannot be separated from patience. Patience is the demonstration of true faith, as Abraham proved by his example. Not only were he and Sarah very old when the promise of a son was given, but the Lord required them to wait many more years until the promise was fulfilled. Instead of being discouraged by the passing of time, their faith in the Lord grew stronger. Then when God finally fulfilled His promise, there was no doubt that *He* had done it.

> **In hope against hope he [Abraham] believed, in order that he might become a father of many nations, according to that which had been spoken, "So shall your descendants be."**

> **And without becoming weak in faith he contemplated his own body, now as good as dead since he was about a hundred years old, and the deadness of Sarah's womb;**

> **yet, with respect to the promise of God, he did not waver in unbelief, but grew strong in faith, giving glory to God,**

> **and being fully assured that what He had promised, He was able also to perform (Romans 4:18-21).**

Patience required that Abraham believe more and more in God for the fulfillment of His promises and less and less in himself. Time is an unfailing test of faith. If our faith is the true faith of God, it will grow stronger, regardless of the circumstances which appear to make fulfillment remote. If it is not true faith, time will erode it. God has ordained that it would take faith *and* patience to inherit His promises. Time will remove that which is not true and strengthen that which is true.

The Lord compared faith to a mustard seed. This is a very tiny seed, yet it can become a large plant and bear fruit. But lest we misunderstand, the seed is *not* the fruit. The seed must be planted, watered, and cultivated to become a healthy plant—only then can it bear fruit. It is the same with faith. That which we interpret as faith is often just the seed planted within us, still needing to be watered and cultivated.

The true faith of God *can* move mountains, raise the dead, and heal the sick. Yet, such maturity and submission to God are required just to *perceive* real faith that the universe is probably quite safe from the foolish interference of immature, though usually well-meaning, Christians. Although it is wonderful and exciting when the Lord performs instantaneous miracles, those which take a little longer are no less miraculous. It amazed the disciples when Jesus turned the water into wine, but the Lord turns water into wine every day—He usually just takes a little longer. It must have been wondrous to see the fig tree wither after the Lord cursed it, but there has never been a tree that withered unless the Lord cursed it; neither has a sickness ever been cured except by His hand.

True faith sees God's hand in everything, regardless of the amount of time He takes or the manner in which

He does His work. Elizabeth Barrett Browning once wrote, "Earth's crammed with heaven, and every common bush afire with God; but only he who sees, takes off his shoes— the rest sit round it and pluck blackberries." True faith is seeing Him and abiding in Him. There are no cheap substitutes or easy formulas for this. It only happens as we grow in our relationship to Him. If we are seeking true faith, we must allow ourselves to be carried well beyond the limits of human ability, so we are cast in utter dependence on *His* ability.

Because many ministries and churches have misunderstood the correlation between faith and patience, there has been a tendency for them to extend their borders beyond what they were called to do. Many also have a mentality that perceives faith as the power of continual expansion. However, true biblical faith may sometimes require us to shrink.

True faith is wonderfully demonstrated by Philip's obedience to leave a city that was stirred with revival to go into the wilderness just to speak with one man. Even though it seems that little was done by Philip from this point on, history testifies that the one man he went to speak with laid the foundation for Christianity in an entire nation. In fact, the long-term fruit of the revival in Samaria is hard to find, but the eunuch's impact on Ethiopia continued for centuries.

If the goals for our ministry are defined by size, we will almost certainly depart from the place of true fruitfulness. When numbers become the motivating force, we tend to depart from the realm of God's grace for us and begin to labor in our own strength. Because of this, many ministry programs and newsletters are increasingly dominated by desperate appeals for money. They claim to be dependent on God's faithfulness, yet they tell us they will be forced to cease operations if they do not hear from *us* soon. We should probably ask, "What would be wrong with that? How would the kingdom of God suffer if that ministry did cease?"

Such pressuring and begging for resources has brought much grief and humiliation to the whole body of Christ. The Lord promised that His seed would not beg for bread (see Psalm 37:25). When He ordains a work, there will be no lack of provision to accomplish it. When Moses asked the people for a contribution to construct the tabernacle, he had to restrain them because they brought too much! When a ministry has to beg, plead, or threaten the body of Christ for its support, there has been a clear departure from the grace of God. When we support such ministries we are only perpetuating their disobedience and presumption.

The scriptural examples of how the Lord prepares His servants are in stark contrast to trends today. After Joseph's dream, it seemed that his life would be marked by only the *opposite* of what had been foretold. After he saw the sun, moon, and stars bowing down to him, Joseph himself became a slave! After finally finding favor with his master, he was sent to the dungeon! According to some popular teachings, Joseph must have been lacking in faith. In reality, though, great faith was nourished in him with each new trial. He knew that to be used for the Lord's purposes, humility came before exaltation: **"Humble yourselves, therefore, under the mighty hand** of God, that He may exalt you *at the proper time"* (I Peter 5:6).

Between the point where we receive the promise and the Promised Land itself, is a wilderness, the exact opposite of what we have been promised. Israel was promised a land flowing with milk and honey, but in her initial wanderings there was not even water! In that place, they were to learn profoundly the fruit of their own striving. When they did finally enter the Promised Land, they were given homes which they did not build, cisterns which they did not dig, and vineyards which they did not plant (see Deuteronomy 6:10-11).

Certainly there were great battles to be fought in that land, but the provision was from God. It has been the "I will" of man that has kept him at enmity with the purposes of God. We will never possess His promises until the "I will" is replaced with "He will," because **he is not served by human hands" (Acts 17:25 NIV)**. The best human intentions and strivings to build for Him will not truly serve His purposes.

Ishmael

Ishmael was the result of Abraham's lapse of patience while waiting for the Lord. After several years of waiting for a son, Abraham began to follow his own reasoning instead of the leading of the Spirit. His wife suggested that the best solution was for him to lie with her maiden. Abraham made a terrible mistake by not seeking the Lord about this; he had relations with Hagar and she conceived and gave birth to Ishmael. As the apostle Paul later pointed out, this child was born after the flesh, not after the Spirit (see Galatians 4:23). Ishmael was of the seed of Cain.

Abraham

The effect of Abraham's lack of patience has been a devastating historical reality. Just as there has been enmity between the Arabs (Ishmael's descendants) and the Jews (Isaac's descendants) since that time, there will always be enmity between that which is born of the flesh and the true seed of God. By the time Isaac was weaned, Ishmael was already mocking him (see Genesis 21:9).

Finally Abraham drove Ishmael out of his house and disallowed his inheritance. A tree can only bear fruit after its own kind. That which is sown in the flesh must be reaped in the flesh. If we revert to the devices of the seed of Cain—even in an attempt to bring about the purposes of God—it will ultimately cause us much trouble.

Abraham was chosen by God to bring about His purposes. The promise he had received from God was true. The consequences of Abraham's self-seeking methods are still wreaking international havoc in the world today. "Ishmaels" brought forth by Christian ministries have been no less devastating to the body of Christ. There is continual conflict between that which is born of the flesh and that which is born of the Spirit.

Because Ishmael was Abraham's son, God blessed him and made him a great nation (see Genesis 17:17-20). The Lord did this even though He knew that Ishmael was going to cause trouble for the promised seed. In the same way, God often blesses our spiritual Ishmaels, causing them to prosper. He will use them as much as He can, and they may bless many people. But when "Isaac" appears, that which was born of the flesh must be driven out. Flesh cannot be an heir with that which is born of the Spirit.

Where flesh and Spirit co-exist, it is inevitable that the flesh will one day persecute that which is born of the

Spirit. The flesh must be maintained by the flesh, through striving, begging, manipulating, and threatening. The more a minister must strive to hold together a work, the more easily intimidated he will be by the appearance of anyone else in his domain. Examples of this are evident throughout the body of Christ. In contrast, the Lord exhorted that we would know the "true seed" by their love for one another.

Chapter 8

LOOKING FOR A CITY

BECAUSE OF GOD'S CALL, ABRAHAM LEFT THE ONLY LAND he had ever known. He did not know where he was going, *but he did know what he was looking for*—**"He was looking for the city which has foundations" (Hebrews 11:10).**

It is the nature of God's call to separate us from all that we have known and built our lives upon. His call is the call to live by faith in Him alone. Only by this faith can we serve Him in a pleasing way (see Hebrews 11:6). His kingdom is not of this world. He is Spirit, and if we are to serve Him we must serve Him in the Spirit. Faith is the door He has provided for us to enter the spiritual realm. As our faith in Him increases, He becomes more real than the world and its forces of influence. Our service to Him will be effective to our degree of single-mindedness; it will be corrupted to the degree that outside influences affect us.

When Jesus was asked by His followers what they needed to do, His answer was pointed: **"This is the work** of God, that you believe in Him whom He has sent" (John 6:29). Our ultimate calling is to believe. But this faith is not blind and it is not naive; it is filled with vision and understanding. Abraham did not know where he was going, but he knew exactly what he was looking for—and so must we. He was looking for a specific city— the one that had "**foundations.**" We have been called to be a part of the same city.

Our calling has foundations; it has substance. The faith we live by also has substance and the "city" we have been called to inhabit has more substance than all the futile works of man. If we settle for less, it is not true faith or the city God has built.

Spiritual Foundations

There is a fundamental principle of construction— the size and strength of any building will be determined by the size and strength of its foundation. If a man is going to build a small house or building, some shallow footings may be sufficient for a foundation. But if he plans to construct a large and strong building, he must do more than just dig footings. He will have to dig deep enough to find the bedrock, and even then he is not finished. He will have to drive pilings into the bedrock and fasten them securely to it. If he does not do this, the building can sink, tilt, or collapse under its own weight.

The same principles apply in spiritual matters. We must build down before we can build up. The amount of patience we have in building down will determine the greatness of that which can be built up. The ruins of ministries, churches, and individuals who failed to lay the proper foundations testify to the soberness of this issue.

Looking for a City

Albert Einstein once made an observation that may be more important than his theory of relativity. He stated simply but profoundly that, "Premature responsibility breeds superficiality." The Lord Jesus testified to this also. He said that seeds which sprout too fast will have shallow roots. Contrary to this wisdom, we often esteem most highly those who develop the fastest. The result has been a serious weakening of many in the body of Christ.

It is crucial that we take the time and energy to lay the foundation properly, but it will be of little use if we do not lay the *right* foundation. Soon after my conversion I found myself in a congregation that emphasized the revelation of the body of Christ. This is an exciting and important revelation, and I began to build my foundation on it. I added many other aspects of Christian truth to my life, but my emphasis was the church. My "building" became bigger and bigger, and my ministry grew rapidly...then the whole thing began to tilt! I knew something was awry, but could not figure out what it was. Everything seemed scriptural, and there was no major sin in my life, but I had to strive more and more to keep everything from falling apart.

Through wise counsel, the Lord revealed my foundational principles as true and right, but they were supposed to be a part of the *building*, not the foundation! I had been building upon the *things* of the Lord instead of upon the Lord Himself. I was worshiping the temple of the Lord, the church, instead of the Lord of the temple. This had caused me to drift into extremes. The apostle Paul explained:

> **For no man can lay a foundation other than the one which is laid, *which is Jesus Christ* (I Corinthians 3:11).**

There Were Two Trees in the Garden

As wonderful as the revelations of God are, there is only ONE foundation—Jesus. If we build upon any other spiritual truth, it will never sustain the pressures of spiritual life. Sooner or later it will crumble and fall apart.

Many doctrines being taught today have drifted into extremes. Often these doctrines began as timely revelations, and in most cases the errors made were not inherent in the doctrines. The problem was in trying to build upon improper foundations. Some people have managed through sheer tenacity to get pretty far along before the whole structure collapsed. Others have recognized early on that something was wrong and have wisely started over with the right foundation.

Often the specific emphasis of a congregation is found to be its foundation. The apostles and preachers of the New Testament had only one message: Jesus. They preached all the doctrines preached today and maybe a few more—yet their whole message was based on the One **"in whom are hidden all the treasures of wisdom and knowledge" (Colossians 2:3).** In a broader sense, Jesus is not only the foundation, He is the whole building! All things are to be summed up in Him. Spiritual maturity is not just growing in the knowledge of certain spiritual truths: **"we are to grow up in all aspects *into Him*" (Ephesians 4:15).**

The apostles' labor was devoted to Christ being formed in His people. There is a major difference between this and trying to get people to conform to certain spiritual truths. The historian, Will Durant, noted the difference between Jesus and Caesar: Caesar sought to change men by changing laws and institutions; Jesus changed laws and institutions by changing men.

Emphasizing externals may bring about a form of godliness, but actually denies God's power. Any emphasis that takes precedence over the Person of Jesus will lead to lifeless ritual. We must see everything through Him. When we try to see Him through the lens of our own doctrines, our view of Him will be distorted.

When the multitudes became hungry, Jesus gave them what they were seeking. He took loaves, broke them, and gave them to the people. After they had eaten, only fragments remained (see John 6:11-12). This is, in a sense, a picture of the church. We have partaken of many different loaves (or emphases), and all that has been left are fragments. Just as Jesus sought to turn the attention of the multitude to the one Loaf, Himself, so He is seeking to turn our attention from varied doctrines to Him. **"In Him all things hold together" (Colossians 1:17).**

In Christ all valid doctrines are found in perfect harmony. When taught as isolated extremes, even the greatest spiritual truths will leave the church in fragments. Seen through Him, all doctrines take their appropriate perspective and balance, and can be taught without creating division. **"God, after He spoke long ago to the fathers in the prophets in many portions and in many ways** [the loaves], *in these last days has spoken to us in His Son* [the one Loaf]…" (Hebrews 1:1-2).**

We see this truth illustrated again in Martha's reaction to the death of her brother Lazarus. Martha accurately understood the doctrine of resurrection. She knew that her brother would rise again on the last day, but her hope was in the *doctrine* of the resurrection, not in Jesus. He redirected her hope, saying, **"I *am* the resurrection" (John 11:25).** But He is not *just* the resurrection: He is the Truth; He is *all* truth. He is the revelation from God and of God. He is "*I AM.*"

If doctrine becomes our emphasis, we are being led astray. We are not changed by doctrine; we are changed by seeing Jesus (see II Corinthians 3:18). Even though anointed teachings are essential to nourish the nature of Christ being formed within each of us, whenever a truth becomes our focus, it will distract us. For this reason, Satan often comes as an angel of light or "messenger of truth." Truth can deceive us. Only in *the* Truth, Jesus, is there life. He did not come just to teach us truth; He came to *be* Truth.

In Exodus 33:8-11, we see Moses speaking to the Lord in the tent of meeting. A pillar of cloud would descend and the Lord would speak to Moses face to face, just as a man speaks to his friend. It was such an awesome sight that all the people would arise and stand at the doorways of their tents to worship when this meeting took place. When Moses returned to the camp, Joshua (who was at that time Moses' personal servant) would remain in the tent of meeting. Joshua was staying to develop his *own* relationship to the Lord. Being the most intimate associate of a man of God was not enough for Joshua—*he had to know the Lord for himself*. It may have been for this reason that Joshua was chosen to lead Israel into the Promised Land.

When we have a great man or woman of God to relate to, there is a danger of becoming spiritually lulled. Because of this, many of the great moves of God in institutions, schools, churches, and missions end with the death of their founders. After Joshua died, it only took Israel one generation to fall into spiritual decadence.

Likewise, few revivals or movements last more than a generation after the initial move of the Spirit. The primary reason for this is that men (or doctrine) becomes the foundation upon which the movement is based. Only when Jesus is the foundation will a move of the Spirit last. The Spirit came to testify of Jesus, not His ministers or doctrines—but Jesus! When we turn to anything else, we will quickly head down side alleys that will never lead us to life.

Before Jesus sent anyone out to minister, He first called them to Himself (see Mark 3:13-14). He did not send them to the finest Bible college or make them take a correspondence course. He said, **"Follow Me."** The light in Him was to become the light in them. This is still His call to those who would be His disciples: **"Follow Me."** We must respond to Him as the Shulammite maid did in the Song of Solomon, who is a type of the bride of Christ.

Tell me, O you whom my soul loves, where do you pasture *your flock*…for why should I be like one who *veils herself* beside the flocks of your companions? (Song of Solomon 1:7)

Jesus *alone* is the mediator between God and man (see I Timothy 2:5). **"Christ is the head of every man" (I Corinthians 11:3).** The leaders and ministers He gives to His church are never meant to take His place; they are given to lead us to Him. The Lord has ordained elders and pastors, but they are exhorted to **"shepherd the *flock of God"* (I Peter 5:2),** not to set up their own flocks.

Throughout the history of the church, there have been those who became veils between the Lord and His people by seeking to establish believers as their own flocks. Foreseeing this, the Lord promised that when He brought His people together they would be **"one flock with one Shepherd"** (John 10:16). The ministry of those who are true under-shepherds is not to establish their own authority over the Lord's people, but His authority. Those who have used this ministry to establish their own domains are disregarding the clear warning of the Chief Shepherd:

> **But do not be called Rabbi; for One is your Teacher, and you are all brothers.**

> **And do not call anyone on earth your father; for One is your Father, He who is in heaven.**

> **And do not be called leaders; for One is your Leader, that is, Christ.**

> **But the greatest among you shall be your servant.**

> **And whoever exalts himself shall be humbled; and whoever humbles himself shall be exalted (Matthew 23:8-12).**

True Ministry

John the Baptist is a wonderful type or model of true ministry. The focus of his entire mission was to reveal Jesus. It was his delight to decrease as Jesus increased. Because of that humility, he was greatly exalted by the Lord Himself, who declared John to be the greatest man ever born of woman (see Matthew 11:11). When we have seen and borne witness to the Son of God as John did, it is a delight to decrease in our ministry as He increases. All spiritual labor is for the purpose of Christ being formed in His people and there is no greater joy than seeing this take place. It is the seal and testimony that we have been abiding in the Vine so as to bear fruit. The true friends of the Bridegroom rejoice to see His day, even if it means the end of their own ministries.

When John the Baptist saw Jesus passing by, he exhorted his disciples to **"Behold, the Lamb of God!"** (John 1:36) Hearing this, John and Andrew left the Baptist and began to follow Jesus. When the Lord perceived them following, He turned and asked them what may be the most important question we could ever consider: **"What do you seek?" (verse 38)** This is one question we will all be required to answer sooner or later. Why are *we* following Him?

John and Andrew answered with another question, but it was possibly the most appropriate reply: "Lord, where do you dwell?" (see verse 38) Hearing this, Jesus beckoned them to do what has been the heart's desire of every true seeker of God since Enoch: **"Come, and you will see" (verse 39).** We do not have to settle for reading about it or hearing the testimonies of those who have experienced intimacy with God; Jesus came to bid each of us to follow Him and see for ourselves where He dwells. This dwelling is not a physical place; He was speaking of the kingdom of God.

The next day Andrew became the first evangelist in history. He found his brother Simon Peter and declared Jesus to be the Messiah (see verses 41 and 42). He did not try to convince Simon with a lengthy discourse from the Scriptures; he did not even share the four spiritual laws with him—he simply **"brought him to Jesus"** **(John 1:42).**

If we are led to Jesus, and not just to the church or to a doctrine, we have come to the only true foundation. Then, like Peter's faith, our faith will grow. Peter was an uneducated, simple fisherman, yet he stood before the most powerful and educated men of his nation and astonished them with his authority and dignity. Peter's faith was not built upon a teaching or the participation in an institution—*he knew Jesus*. There is no formula given for salvation—it is a Person. Truth is not just a systematic theology—it is Jesus. He came to be our Life. He is the deepest desire of the human heart. Only in Him do we really begin to live.

Chapter 9

JACOB AND ESAU, REUBEN AND JOSEPH

**I have loved Jacob; but I have hated Esau…
(Malachi 1:2-3).**

UNDERSTANDING THIS SCRIPTURE HAS BEEN DIFFICULT FOR many believers. Why would the Lord favor a lying, cheating, deceiving schemer like Jacob over a nice guy like Esau, who loved and obeyed his parents and seemed to be a godly man? This seems incongruous. But God does not look at the outward character; He looks on the heart.

Esau may have had a strong external character, but he was weak in spirit. He proved to be more concerned about the immediate gratification of his appetite than about his eternal inheritance in Christ. He traded his birthright as the firstborn of Isaac for a single bowl of stew! When we recognize what a profound affront this was to God and the value of His calling upon the chosen seed, we should be shocked. But we should be even more shocked when we understand just how prevalent this same nature is within most of us today.

The Lord Jesus purchased with His own blood the opportunity for us to come boldly before the very throne of God. Like Esau, we, too, often disregard this privilege for the immediate gratification of our flesh! How often do we spend more time each day before worthless television programs than in the Word of God or in prayer? A multitude of other distractions can easily keep us from even the most basic spiritual disciplines—distractions that are often worth even less than the stew! How can we cast stones at Esau? How many of us live lives that are just as much an affront to the grace of God? Are we thoughtlessly trading away our eternal birthright in Christ for temporary, carnal gratification?

Wrestling with God

In contrast to Esau, Jacob so highly valued the birthright that he risked his life to attain it. In many ways, he may have been more carnal than Esau, yet his heart burned for this spiritual inheritance. He was determined to obtain God's blessing, even if he had to wrestle with God to get it (see Genesis 32:24-32).

To wrestle with God in rebellion is folly. To wrestle with Him for our inheritance requires a determination He longs to see in us. Jacob determined that he was going to lay hold of the Lord and not let Him go until he had received the blessing. How contrary this is to the way we often seek the Lord! The Lord exhorts through Jeremiah: **"and you will seek Me and find Me,** *when you search for Me with all your heart"* **(Jeremiah 29:13).**

Even though the Lord wants us to seek Him and *find* Him, He would be doing us a great disservice if His blessings were too easily attained. This would only feed our slothfulness. He often makes Himself difficult to find so we will have to search for Him more diligently.

In a way, the Lord is like the parent who teaches his child to walk by backing away so the child will have to take more steps to reach him. He wants to bring us to the place where we are seeking Him all the time with all our hearts. But instead of taking more steps to reach Him, we often give up and sit down, thus not reaching Him at all.

The Lord does not want us to stop seeking Him until we find Him. He wants to answer all of our prayers. The answer may be "no," but we should never stop seeking Him until we have heard from Him. Silence is not an answer to prayer. If He were to answer some of our half-hearted prayers, it would be detrimental to our spiritual growth. We must not give up until we have found Him.

Jacob would not give up seeking the blessing, and he received it. Not only did he receive the blessing he sought, his nature was changed as well. To signify this, the Lord changed his name from Jacob, which means "usurper," to Israel, which means "a prince with God." All this happened because Jacob had **striven with God and with men and** [had] **prevailed" (Genesis 32:28).** If we persistently seek the Lord, we, too, will find Him. As in the case of Jacob, our nature will be changed from that of Cain to the nature of God's Son. Then we, too, will be "princes with God."

Reuben, Jacob's firstborn, had the same nature as his uncle Esau. He allowed his flesh to rob him of his inheritance when his carnal appetite drove him to defile his father's bed. When Jacob blessed his sons before passing away, he only had a rebuke for Reuben.

> **Reuben, you are my first-born; my might and the beginning of my strength. Preeminent in dignity and preeminent in power.**
>
> ***Uncontrolled as water*, you shall not have preeminence, because you went up to your father's bed... (Genesis 49:3-4).**

Like Esau, Reuben may have been preeminent in dignity and power, but he was ruled by his flesh and it cost him dearly. The lack of self-control began in the Garden and is still today robbing many of their eternal inheritance in Christ.

Satan's Food

In the Scriptures, dust is often symbolic of the carnal nature of man or the "flesh" as it is sometimes referred to (Adam's flesh was made from the dust). The curse upon the serpent was that he would eat the dust (see Genesis 3:14), signifying that Satan was to feed on the carnal nature of man. Satan's dominion over man is perpetuated by man's carnal nature.

Since the Garden, one of Satan's most successful tactics for robbing God's people of their inheritance has been to offer them the immediate gratification of their flesh. This tactic has been so successful that Satan even tried it on Jesus. Knowing that Jesus was to be the heir of the world, but also knowing of the testing and consecration required before the fulfillment of God's promises could be received, he proposed an easier way. Satan proposed that if Jesus would bow down and worship him, he would give Him the world *immediately*. This way He would not have to go to the cross; He would not have to suffer, and to appease one of the most difficult trials of the flesh, He would not have to wait.

By this same seductive deception, Satan has induced many saints to take the "easy" way to their ultimate consternation. The invitation to worship Satan is seldom blatant enough to be perceived as such—it is usually simply an invitation to take the wider, more traveled path. The way of God is a very narrow, difficult path, and there are no shortcuts. **"Through many tribulations we must enter the kingdom of God" (Acts 14:22).**

Many teachings have suggested easier ways, but such ways do not lead to the kingdom. To walk with God is to walk against the tide of the whole human race, and when a man walks against the tide, he is bound to make waves. As we have clearly been told: **"all who desire to live godly in Christ Jesus will be persecuted" (II Timothy 3:12).** Satan is forever inducing us to relax and flow with the tide to avoid persecution and misunderstanding. Only those who love their calling more than they love comfort and acceptance will stand.

Although the church has been decimated by a lack of discipline and self-control, a problem possibly more destructive has been our uncanny willingness to accept weak spiritual leaders. We do this because they usually appear, like Reuben, to be "preeminent in dignity and strength." Paul observed this tendency in the Corinthian church: **"For you bear with anyone if he enslaves you, if he devours you, if he takes advantage of you, if he exalts himself, if he hits you in the face" (II Corinthians 11:20).** Carnal men respond to carnal strength.

Just as Israel foolishly sought a king they could see, hear, and touch in place of God whom they could not see, we have often done the same. Like Israel, we also have tended to be quick to follow anyone who appears to be head and shoulders above others. Because of this, we have also suffered almost continuous defeat, humiliation, and the loss of God's manifest glory and presence.

To judge by externals is a common error, and it is a great temptation even for those who are intimate with the Lord. The great prophet Samuel had a difficult time learning this lesson. It is surprising that after the fiasco with Saul, he would be so quick to judge another potential king by physical appearance. Nevertheless, after the Lord sent him to the house of Jesse to anoint a successor, he succumbed to the same temptation:

> **Then it came about when they entered, that he looked at Eliab and thought, "Surely the LORD's anointed is before Him."**
>
> **But the LORD said to Samuel, "Do not look at his appearance or at the height of his stature, because I have rejected him; for God sees not as man sees, for man looks at the outward appearance, but the LORD looks at the heart" (I Samuel 16:6-7).**

Many who are "preeminent in dignity and strength" are "uncontrolled as water" and weak in spiritual strength. The Lord's strength is made perfect in weakness (see II Corinthians 12:9). **"God has chosen the weak things of the world to shame the things which are strong" (I Corinthians 1:27).** Neither natural strengths nor intellectual and social prowess are requirements for spiritual leadership. Such qualities may even be hindrances.

This is not to advocate that we should only look for the physically weak or intellectually slow to be our spiritual leaders, but we should not judge by externals—period! It is critical that we be sensitive to the Spirit as to whom He has chosen. Natural abilities cannot bring forth the fruit of the Spirit. He often chooses the weak or slow so His perfect wisdom and power may be evidenced.

> **For we are the true circumcision, who worship in the Spirit of God and glory in Christ Jesus and *put no confidence in the flesh* (Philippians 3:3).**

The Lord declared through the prophet Isaiah the demeanor of those He would choose:

> **Thus says the LORD, "Heaven is My throne, and the earth is My footstool. Where then is a house you could build for Me? And where is a place that I may rest?**

> **"For My hand made all these things, thus all these things came into being," declares the LORD. *"But to this one I will look* [to be His habitation], *to him who is humble and contrite of spirit, and who trembles at My word"* (Isaiah 66:1-2).**

True humility is a prerequisite for being a vessel of the Lord. It was the pride of man that allowed him to presume he could be like God. It is this same pride which continues to separate us from Him. When we see Him as He is, this presumption is stopped cold. The clamoring of the world's great and mighty seem pitiful and absurd when we see the Lord in His glory.

The world's most righteous men are utterly humiliated when they behold the Lord. The "greatest man born of a woman" did not consider himself worthy to even untie His shoes. Where is the house that we can build for Him? The greatest human talent cannot accomplish His work. Only the Spirit can beget that which is Spirit. He does not call us for our strengths—He calls us for our weaknesses. Just as our Lord Jesus emptied Himself to become a servant, He looks for those who will have no confidence in the flesh and will become vessels for His Spirit.

Because of the pride of man, the Lord places His treasure in that which is repulsive to the proud. Even Jesus, the Lord and Creator of the universe, was birthed in a stable and reared in the most despised town in the most despised nation on earth. Prophetically we were told, **"He has no stately form or majesty that we should look upon Him, nor appearance that we should be attracted to Him" (Isaiah 53:2).** To receive Him in this way, we have to renounce our pride. That is the point.

The Lord is seeking those who are not attracted by externals, but by the Spirit. Men in their pride have rejected the One who is the very cornerstone of creation. To the degree that we follow our pride (or trust in the carnal abilities of man), we will reject Him. If we are to be the sons of God, we must be led by the Spirit of God. **"Therefore, from now on we recognize no man according to the flesh..." (II Corinthians 5:16).**

Reuben, Jacob's firstborn, abounded in outward strength and dignity, but lacked inner fortitude. Joseph was Jacob's next to youngest son. Although despised by his brothers, God had chosen him to inherit the birthright of the firstborn:

> **Now the sons of Reuben the first-born of Israel (for he was the first-born, but because he defiled his father's bed, his birthright was given to the sons of Joseph the son of Israel; so that he is not enrolled in the genealogy according to the birthright.**
>
> **Though Judah prevailed over his brothers, and from him came the leader, yet the birthright belonged to Joseph) (I Chronicles 5:1-2).**

Reuben committed the detestable act of lying with his father's wife, which cost him his birthright. In contrast, Joseph remained faithful, even under the most tempting of circumstances. He refused the advances of his master's wife even though it meant imprisonment. This took place after Joseph had already suffered incredible personal injustices. In a land that was void of the most basic moral standards, he faced situations which would have weakened any person's resolve. But Joseph had a law in his heart that was stronger than external circumstances and temptations. As a type of the Messiah who was to come, Joseph was rejected by his brothers, but became the very cornerstone of their salvation.

Body, Soul, and Spirit

Man is basically made up of three parts: body, soul, and spirit. The body is composed of the elements of the earth. As the popular statement contends: "We are what we eat." To maintain a healthy body, we need a proper diet and proper exercise. However, our natural tendency is toward junk food, which does not satisfy the basic nutritional needs of our bodies. We also tend to be lazy and not exercise. Discipline is required to maintain a healthy diet and proper exercise.

The soul of man is composed of the intellect, emotions, and will. The soul, like the body, is going to become what we feed it. It, too, has a tendency to desire "junk food" and to get out of shape. Every seed that is sown in our minds will be reaped (see Galatians 6:7). What we allow ourselves to read, think, hear, or see is critical to our soul's health. We must be disciplined to seek the proper intellectual exercise and diet.

In contrast to the body and soul, the spirit of regenerated man has a tendency toward God. Yet it, too, must have proper diet and exercise. Jesus said, **"The words that I have spoken to you are spirit and are life" (John 6:63).** His words are our spiritual food. Because man was created to have fellowship with God, there is a spiritual void in his life until that fellowship with God is restored. But just as a man deprived of nutritious food will readily gobble junk food, a man denied the proper spiritual diet will fill his hunger with that which is of an evil spirit. For this reason, those who claim to be materialists—starting off with no belief in the supernatural at all—often fall to the most base forms of spiritualism and the occult.

The spiritual void in us causes all men to gravitate toward the supernatural. Man was created to have fellowship with God, who is Spirit. Consequently, a relationship to the supernatural is "natural" for men. But if we do not know the true power of God, we will be in danger of being duped by the supernatural power of the enemy. This is why the apostle Paul explained that his message and preaching **"were not in persuasive words of wisdom, but in demonstration of the Spirit and of power, that your faith should not rest on the wisdom of men, but on the power of God"** (I Corinthians 2:4-5).

The Scriptures testify that as we draw near the end of this age, the spiritual conflict will become increasingly supernatural. Our protection against being led astray by the deceptive power of the enemy is not to reject all supernatural power, but to know the true power of God. The hunger in men for the supernatural will be filled. If the church does not provide the genuine power of God, men will fall for the counterfeit.

The spiritually weak are ruled by their bodies—impulses, habits, and fleshly desires control them. We could include Esau and Reuben in this category. Others are ruled by their souls—their emotions, feelings, and opinions. But the Lord has called us to walk by the *Spirit*. **"For all who are being led by the Spirit of God, these are sons of God"** (Romans 8:14). The Lord desires for us to have a healthy body, soul, and spirit subjected to His Spirit.

When we first commit ourselves to the Lord, we inevitably emphasize correction in areas of our lives that belong to the body and soul. In most cases there are problems in these areas which do need immediate attention. However, the body and soul are not meant to be the focus of our attention. Before becoming Christians, most of us were totally unaware of the spiritual aspect of our constitution. Sadly, many Christians go through life almost completely ignorant of their spiritual nature. The emphasis of much teaching concerning spiritual growth actually has focused much more on the soul realm—knowledge, wisdom, understanding, and discipline of the will. Even though these are critical areas, there is much more to our life in Christ!

> **But an hour is coming, and now is, when the true worshipers shall worship the Father in spirit and truth; for such people the Father seeks to be His worshipers.**

> **God is spirit; and those who worship Him must worship in spirit and truth (John 4:23-24).**

The Lord said His words are *spirit* and life. He also said, **"When he puts forth all his own, he goes before them, and the sheep follow him *because they know his voice*"** (John 10:4). If we are His sheep, we must know His voice. This is possibly the most important aspect of our lives—to know His voice. As He said, His sheep follow Him **"*because* they know his voice"** (John 10:4).

Those led by the Spirit of God are the sons of God. We are not to be led by impulses, feelings, or reasonings. There is a straight and narrow path that leads to true life. Even if we strive to follow all the principles found in the Bible, if we do so on the basis of human strength and reasoning we will still end up far from the will of God. It is crucial for those who are His to know His voice and be led by His Spirit.

Chapter 10
PHARAOH, MOSES, AND SPIRITUAL AUTHORITY

PHARAOH IS A TYPE OR BIBLICAL MODEL OF SATAN, THE present ruler of this age. He is another personification of the seed of the serpent. In him we see many of the same devices that Satan uses to keep God's people in bondage. We also see in Pharaoh an example of oppressive authority rooted in the selfish ambitions of the rebellious nature.

Moses, on the other hand, is a type of Christ who has come to set God's people free. As he prophetically explained to Israel, **"The LORD your God will raise up for you a prophet** *like me* **from among you, from your countrymen, you shall listen to him" (Deuteronomy 18:15).** He was explaining that his life was a foreshadowing of The Prophet, Jesus, who was to come.

We can easily see the parallels in the lives of Moses and Jesus. When Moses was born, Pharaoh issued a decree to destroy all the male children born to Israel (see Exodus 1:22). Herod, in a similar way, sought to destroy Jesus by having all the male children in Bethlehem killed. The first time Moses revealed himself to his people, they rejected him as their deliverer, just as Jesus was rejected the first time He came to Israel. The second time Moses came, it was with great power, foreshadowing Jesus' return. There are many other examples in the life and ministry of Moses that were prophetic parallels of Jesus. In Moses we also have a wonderful example of the self-sacrificing nature of true spiritual authority, as opposed to the self-seeking nature of human authority.

Under Pharaoh's dominion Israel was in slavery and subjected to toil. In contrast, the Lord sent Moses to set Israel free and bring them into a land flowing with milk and honey that they might find rest. This illustrates a clear difference between the kingdom of this world and the kingdom of God. One kingdom is seeking to increase the bondage of its subjects, while the other seeks to set men free.

In this world, little is accomplished without toil. This is not speaking of *labor*, for man labored in the Garden (cultivated it) before the fall. The curse of *toil*, on the other hand, was the result of transgression (see Genesis 2:15). Toil is work that is accomplished only with *great and painful* effort. We labor in the kingdom of God, but the Lord's yoke is easy and His burden is light. In His kingdom more work is accomplished with less effort. All toil brings weariness, but labor energized by Christ, regardless of whether it is a secular or spiritual endeavor, brings rest and refreshment:

> **Take My yoke upon you, and learn from Me, for I am gentle and humble in heart;** *and you shall find rest for your souls* **(Matthew 11:29).**

The attempts of Satan to enslave us are often very subtle; at times they even have the appearance of liberty. But the "freedom" of this world always leads to bondage: **"promising them freedom while they themselves are slaves of corruption; for by what a man is overcome, by this he is enslaved" (II Peter 2:19).** The present trend toward sexual license is a good example of this. The more "free" one becomes in his pursuit of satisfaction, the less satisfaction he experiences. Soon this "freedom" becomes a compulsion to seek satisfaction in new and different experiences. These only increase the appetite while providing less and less fulfillment, until only perversions seem interesting. Then the degree of perversion must be increased until one is ultimately consumed and destroyed, seeking satisfaction.

In Christ the opposite is true. What externally appears to be bondage is what actually sets us free. He created the sexual appetite of man to be fulfilled. One of the very first things that the Lord said was not good was for man to be alone. He declared man's need for companionship when He said that He created woman to correspond (literally, "fit together") with man (see Genesis 2:18). The fitting together is not just physical, but encompasses soul and spirit as well. Sexual intercourse is only one level of interrelation that the Lord designated between man and woman. All of them lead to UNION. The Lord instituted marriage and prohibited sexual intercourse outside of marriage so we would experience the fulfillment we are truly seeking—union in spirit, soul, and body.

Whenever we enter into sexual intercourse with selfish motives, we are even more alone than we were before. The loneliness increases our appetite for union, which is usually translated into a need for more sexual intercourse. Lust is a self-perpetuating cycle that becomes more intense as it continues. Sexual intercourse that is born out of love and *commitment* to the union profoundly helps to enhance the relationship.

Of course, marriage does not guarantee the proper use of this gift, but sex is *never* utilized properly outside of marriage. Through the union experienced in marriage, we begin to understand the greater union of Christ and His church and the yearning of our spirits to be joined with Him. Our union with Him brings us satisfaction and fulfillment which the world cannot comprehend. This is the fulfillment of the purpose for which we were created.

Everything pertaining to life and godliness is provided for us in Christ (see II Peter 1:3). We can only be fulfilled in Him. Every evil is the perversion of a God-given gift, caused by man's attempt to find fulfillment and security outside of Christ. This only leads to dissatisfaction and insecurity. Loneliness is a root of much evil. Within all men there is the need to fit, to be united with the Lord and His creation. The kingdom of God is the ultimate symphony—the harmony of the Creator with His creation.

The essential need to be harmonious is basic to all creation, but man has distorted this by determining to seek fulfillment on his own. The more removed one becomes from overall harmony, the more self-assertive he will become, further disrupting the harmony. Those who attain power or authority in this manner will inevitably become paranoid and insecure, increasingly threatened by anyone they cannot control. Until God's kingdom comes, men will incessantly form clubs and societies in order to "feel a part" and to have a place where they can strive for rank and recognition.

Those who have become truly united with Christ and His purposes will have no need for the recognition of rank or position. Those who are properly joined to Christ are also joined to His body and will be rightly fitted together in their pre-ordained places. To be known by God eventually erases any need to be recognized by others. To the believer who has found fulfillment in Him, there is equal willingness to become the least or greatest. Rank is not important—fruit is. For the redeemed, united purpose will greatly overshadow personal position.

More on the Fear of Rejection

We discussed this a bit previously, but we need to look at it in more depth. When man has not been redeemed and then united with Christ, he carries the rejection of Cain. Man is not acceptable to God except through Jesus. Just as Cain's sacrifice of his own works was rejected, people propagated through Cain know deep inside that they are not acceptable to God. Fear of rejection is probably the most dominant force within those who have not been "crucified with Christ."

It is not good for man to be alone, yet this fear of rejection causes people to shy away from the very thing they need for fulfillment. Fear causes man to put up façades of independence and self-sufficiency to protect himself from possible rejection. Often these façades cause rejection, which produces more aloofness. It is a vicious and self-perpetuating cycle.

Cain was rejected because he sought God on his own terms. This same presumption caused the perversion of man's spirit in the first place. After the Fall, this attitude prevailed, deeply rooted in disharmony. The insecure are threatened by that which they cannot control. As man is further removed from what he needs most (union), insecurity increases. Relationships are reduced to devices used to manipulate and control. They are not unions but wars, often held together by the greater fear of being left completely alone. When we enter a union with terms that demand our control, those terms prohibit true union.

True union cannot take place while self-seeking and self-preservation are involved. These are barriers that will separate us from one another and the Lord. True union requires the total giving of oneself to the other. Only when we lay down all barriers and façades in order to give are we really open to receive. We must first lose our lives if we are to find them.

In Christ, the rejection of Cain is removed. In Him we come to know God's acceptance, which is greater than any other. In His love we are secure. We are able to trust Him because His cross proved that He has our best interests in mind. As we become secure in His lordship and control, the compulsion to control other people and circumstances is reduced until we are ultimately able to enter the "Sabbath rest" of God. Only then are we truly fit to serve in positions of authority.

When fear controls us, every other perception is distorted. Until there is restoration of union with God, man is utterly alone. He may have relationships with others, but true union is not possible until the perfect love of God has cast out all of his fears (see I John 4:18).

To the fearful, the world is a threat and life is a battle to gain control. When the fearful gain control of a situation, the result is oppression. Fear causes overreactions to real or perceived threats to one's position.

There is an old adage that states, "Power corrupts; absolute power corrupts absolutely." This is true for those who seek authority, but have not come under the authority of Christ. The lust for power is fueled by the insecurity of man. His drive for control is often a defense mechanism to protect him from rejection. But power over others will never allay fears; it will only increase them. The more we strive to maintain dominion over our little kingdoms, the greater the burdens become. It is only when we have "lost our lives" (our claims to dominion) and surrendered dominion to Christ that we find life and freedom.

All who achieve power without knowing the love of God are open to paranoia. The smallest deviation from doctrine or the smallest expression of free-thinking becomes absurdly sinister. Those who have truly surrendered to Christ will not be intimidated by challenges or dismayed by rejection. Those who exercise authority with selfish motives are corrupt, regardless of pretentious piety. Leaders secure in Christ will handle authority with the greatest care, knowing they are His servants.

Submitting to Delegated Authority

We see a typical reaction of Cain's seed in Pharaoh. When Moses sought freedom for Israel, Pharaoh made the burdens on his slaves heavier (see Exodus 5:9). With every attempt at freedom by underlings, those of the seed of Cain will become more oppressive, and their fears more irrational. There is inherent corruption in any authority apart from God.

The Lord created man to rule over the fish of the sea, the birds of the air, and every living thing that creeps on the earth (see Genesis 1:28), but it was not originally His purpose for men to rule over other men. He alone was to be man's authority. When man resisted His rule and chose to go his own way, the Lord established men over other men to keep the world from being reduced to utter chaos. For this reason, the apostles exhorted the church to be subject to all earthly authority.

> **Let every person be in subjection to the governing authorities. For there is no authority except from God, and those which exist are established by God.**

> **Therefore he who resists authority has opposed the ordinance of God; and they who have opposed will receive condemnation upon themselves.**

> **For rulers are not a cause of fear for good behavior, but for evil. Do you want to have no fear of authority? Do what is good and you will have praise from the same;**

> **for it is a minister of God to you for good. But if you do what is evil, be afraid; for it does not bear the sword for nothing; for it is a minister of God, an avenger who brings wrath upon the one who practices evil (Romans 13:1-4).**

Pharaoh, Moses, and Spiritual Authority

Submit yourselves *for the Lord's sake* **to every human institution, whether to a king as the one in authority,**

or to governors as sent by him for the punishment of evildoers and the praise of those who do right (I Peter 2:13-14).

Even though there have been many dictators, kings, and presidents in which the spirit of evil has been apparent, no one is established in authority unless God allows it. We may not understand the Lord's purpose in many things, but every one He permits to come to power will in some way bring about His purposes, even if it is as a judgment for a people's transgression. Since God is well aware of the inherent corruption in power exercised by the unredeemed, He exhorts His people to pray for all who are in authority. If we, without God's grace, were subject to the same pressures and temptations as those in authority, we would stumble terribly. Earthly rulers should receive our support even when others desert them.

This is certainly not to propose that if the Nazis were to come to power again we should attend their rallies and give them our allegiance. Obviously there are exceptions to the principle of obeying those in positions of authority. When the Sanhedrin demanded that the apostles stop preaching in the name of Jesus, their reply was, **"We must obey God rather than men"** (**Acts 5:29**). God may overrule all authority of men. When man's authority is in conflict with God's, we must obey Him first. This is, however, the only time we should disobey established authorities.

Even though King Saul had become oppressed by an evil spirit and God declared that He was going to remove him, David was smitten with guilt when he merely cut off the edge of Saul's robe! No matter that Saul was trying to kill him! David's fear of touching someone ordained by the Lord was greater than any personal resentment or ambition. He had already been anointed king in Saul's place, yet David refused to take this authority by his own hand. David's faith in the Lord's righteous judgment and perfect ways is a primary reason the Lord promised him that his kingdom would endure forever. Had he grasped the authority by his own hand, he would have been subject to equal retribution; we will reap what we sow.

To the degree we strive in our own strength to attain even that which God has appointed for us, our ultimate authority is weakened in the same measure. Though the authority of the world is subject to the corruption of fallen man, we must submit ourselves to it "for conscience sake" (the same conscience that smote David for touching Saul's robe). We may have to disobey civil authorities under certain circumstances, but we are not to oppose them, because **"God is the Judge; He puts down one, and exalts another" (Psalm 75:7).**

Leadership God's Way

Though God did not originally ordain men to rule over men, it will be necessary until His kingdom has been restored. The primary purpose of the Church Age is the testing and refining of those faithful followers who will rule with Him over men in the age to come. This reign is to last a thousand years (see Revelation 20:4), at which time all things will again have been made subject to Him (see I Corinthians 15:28). After the thousand-year day of the Lord is completed, **"and they shall not teach again, each man his neighbor and each man his brother, saying, 'Know the LORD,' for they shall all know Me, from the least of them to the greatest of them, declares the LORD"** (Jeremiah 31:34).

This was the original plan, that we would all know the Lord intimately and be responsible to Him; and this is the condition to which man will return. All authority the Lord establishes for and through His people is toward this end. This is not speaking of authority that is established to keep order until the kingdom of God comes; that authority is fundamentally different and is established to bring about different ends, as the Lord Jesus explained:

...**"You know that the rulers of the Gentiles lord it over them, and their great men exercise authority over them.**

"It is not so among you, but whoever wishes to become great among you shall be your servant,

"and whoever wishes to be first among you shall be your slave;

"just as the Son of Man did not come to be served, but to serve, and to give His life a ransom for many" (Matthew 20:25-28).

In this statement the Lord was not condemning Gentile authority; indeed, He established it! Even so, He made it clear that kingdom authority was of a different nature.

There are two kinds of leaders: those who use people for their own interests and those who sacrifice themselves for the interests of the people. The former denotes the nature of worldly authority; the latter godly authority. Pharaoh allowed his country to be destroyed while striving to preserve his power over the Jews. In Moses, we have a striking contrast to Pharaoh's self-centeredness and a wonderful example of kingdom authority. As Israel continually resisted and rejected him, Moses so loved and identified with these people that he offered his own life to appease God's wrath toward them. Such is the nature of all who are truly exercising authority in the Spirit of Jesus.

> **Have this attitude in yourselves which was also in Christ Jesus,**
>
> **who, although He existed in the form of God, did not regard equality with God a thing to be grasped,**
>
> **but emptied Himself, taking the form of a bond-servant, and being made in the likeness of men.**
>
> **And being found in appearance as a man, He humbled Himself by becoming obedient to the point of death, even death on a cross** [the most humiliating death possible].
>
> **Therefore also God highly exalted Him, and bestowed on Him the name which is above every name,**
>
> **that at the name of Jesus every knee should bow... (Philippians 2:5-10).**

For the seed of Cain, authority is an opportunity for self-promotion and self-exaltation. In Christ, the call to authority is the call to self-sacrifice; it is the call to become a slave and to give up our own interests. To rule in Christ is not self-gratifying; it is self-emptying. In Christ we do not serve in order to make a reputation but to become of **"no reputation"** (see Philippians 2:7 KJV). While Pharaoh was one of the most arrogant of all men, attempting even to fight against God, it was said that Moses was the most humble man on the face of the earth (see Numbers 12:3).

Selfish ambition is one of the most destructive characteristics found in ministry and has led to much of the perversion and humiliation which has come upon the church. When men are established in positions of authority prematurely, it is a tragedy for both the leader and those being led. To be placed in spiritual authority before we are freed from carnality will only feed that nature and may well prevent the development of true leadership gifts. To quote Albert Einstein once again: "Premature responsibility breeds superficiality."

Proper Spiritual Authority

Spiritual authority was a major issue in the body of Christ during the 1970s. Though incorrect interpretations have caused strife and confusion, the issue has challenged many to seek an understanding of the true nature of spiritual authority. One lesson was that we need discernment and patience in waiting for God to establish His authority. A human perspective led Israel to cry for a king—and Saul was the disastrous result. The Lord was going to give Israel a king at the proper time. He had raised up the prophet Samuel specifically to prepare Israel for the coming king, a development that had been prophesied by Jacob (see Genesis 49:10). But the people could not wait for God's chosen time.

Sadly, it seems this is repeated every time the Lord is about to move in a special way. Men begin to perceive a need for something God is preparing them for, but their impatience causes them to press the Lord before His perfect time. For this reason, it seems there has always been a doctrinal Ishmael before Isaac or a Saul before David. Time after time the Lord has chosen the younger son to be the heir of His promises rather than the older, as a testimony that the earthly would always be born before the spiritual.

We only have true spiritual authority to the degree that the King lives within us. Paul said that he waited to begin his ministry until it pleased the Father to reveal His Son *in* him, not just *to* him (see Galatians 1:15-17). In this same discourse, he declared that he did not immediately consult with flesh and blood about the matter. He received his message from the Lord, but only after fourteen years did he go to Jerusalem for confirmation.

"In abundance of counselors there is victory" (Proverbs 11:14). Submission to the body of Christ and the presbytery is important, but over-emphasizing this can dilute true spiritual authority. The essential factor in fruitfulness of ministry is union with the Lord, not union with the body. There are many congregations of professing Christians which claim to be Christ's but are not joined to Him. Paul warned us about ministries **"not holding fast to the Head" (Colossians 2:19).** He gave no warnings about those who were not submitted to the body. This is because one can be joined to the body without having a personal relationship with the Head. But the reverse is not true; one cannot be joined to the Head without also being joined to His body. It is simply a matter of getting our priorities right.

Many "lone rangers" have made glaring failures of their ministries and lives. Some have attributed this to a lack of submission to the authority of the church. To a degree this may be true, but there have been many who were in full submission to church authorities and have fallen just as severely. In contrast, history is filled with testimonies of individuals, completely isolated from fellow believers, who have endured incredible tests and remained faithful. Some doctrines of submission to spiritual authority are actually counterproductive in preparing individuals to be faithful and obedient to the Lord.

This is not to promote the wrong kind of individualism and spiritual independence. But when emphasis on submission to the church exceeds submission to the Lord, there will be tragic consequences as our recent history testifies. Some of the most anointed ministries the Lord has given to His church in our time have been rejected by large portions of the body of Christ because they did not emphasize their body-union as much as their Christ-union. Likewise, some diabolical influences were allowed in because the perpetrators could feign all of the outward appearances of being submissive.

An *over*emphasis on submission to the body will produce a distortion of true discipleship. Spirituality cannot be transferred by osmosis. A clear example of this is the case of Paul and Gamaliel. Since in Acts 22:3 Paul declared himself to have been a disciple of Gamaliel, we might expect him to be like his teacher. However, while Paul was sitting under Gamaliel, we see a great contrast. Gamaliel's counsel to the Sanhedrin, recorded in Acts 5:34-39, contains amazing depth of patience and wisdom. When the rest of the council intended to slay the apostles for teaching in the name of Jesus, Gamaliel wisely suggested that they leave them alone: **"...for if this plan or action should be of men, it will be overthrown; but if it is of God, you will not be able to overthrow them; or else you may even be found fighting against God" (verses 38-39).** But what was Paul's reaction to the young church? **"I persecuted this Way to the death" (Acts 22:4).**

Men cannot change other men. Even the greatest pastor cannot be the Holy Spirit to his people. We may be able to affect outward behavior to some degree, but only the Holy Spirit can change a person's heart. There is a place for discipleship, but molding another person's life is a serious and delicate matter. Some of the greatest mistakes that are commonly made by those in leadership come when we try to take the place of the Holy Spirit in another person's life. There is no rigid recipe for imparting one's life and wisdom to another; it must be a Spirit-ordained and guided relationship.

It has become very easy for a believer to be rightly related to the body (according to the popular interpretation) and have almost no relationship with the Lord. To be rightly related to the Lord is the most important element in every life and ministry. The church cannot save; it cannot heal; it cannot baptize with the Holy Spirit; it cannot lead us into all truth. Only the Lord can do these things. When our emphasis becomes the church more than the Lord, we have been reduced to worshiping the creation instead of the blessed Creator, and our faith has been reduced to a form of godliness which denies the very power of the gospel.

We are not changed by beholding the church; we are changed as we behold the Lord (see II Corinthians 3:18).

Neither will the world be drawn to the Lord by beholding the church—it will be drawn to the Lord when the church begins to lift up the Lord instead of itself. It is only after we have been united with the Lord that there can be a *real* union with His body. In beholding the Head, the body is joined (see Colossians 2:19).

Knowing God's Ways

King David made a profound observation when he declared that the Lord **"made known His ways to Moses, His acts to the sons of Israel" (Psalm 103:7)**. It was not enough for Moses to see the acts of the Lord; he longed to know His ways. This desire led him to become one of the most discerning spiritual leaders of all time. Moses reveals why knowing the Lord's ways are so important:

> **Then Moses said to the LORD, "See, Thou dost say to me, 'Bring up this people!' But Thou Thyself has not let me know whom Thou wilt send with me. Moreover, Thou hast said, 'I have known you by name, and you have also found favor in My sight.'**
>
> **"Now therefore, I pray Thee, if I have found favor in Thy sight, let me know Thy ways, that I may know Thee, so that I may find favor in Thy sight" (Exodus 33:12-13).**

Moses knew that he could only properly lead God's people if he knew His ways, and only in knowing the Lord's ways could he properly know Him. He was called to lead God's people, but he had the wisdom to know they could not be led in the same way other people might be led. The world's ways are not God's ways, and neither can they accomplish the Lord's purposes.

There Were Two Trees in the Garden

This is a most crucial matter for the leadership of the body of Christ to understand. So often we have appointed leaders in the church because of what they have attained in the world. Being a leader in the world may actually hinder spiritual leadership. Natural abilities and talents will mislead us if we depend on them in spiritual matters. That which is flesh is flesh; only that which is born of the Spirit can bring forth that which is Spirit. Of the twelve foundational apostles chosen by the Lord to lead His church into the new age, not one of them had previously been in a position of secular leadership. In fact, it seems they were a unique fraternity of those voted "least likely to succeed."

The author of Hebrews explained that because the Israel did not know the ways of the Lord, she was not able to enter His rest (see Hebrews 3:10-11). Being content with only God's blessings, with no concern for really knowing Him, cost Israel her inheritance, just as it will us.

The Promised Land and other blessings that the Lord wanted to give Israel were great, but they were not the reason the Lord brought Israel out of Egypt. Israel was called to be a nation of priests, to serve Him and manifest to all the peoples of the earth the character of her Creator (see Exodus 19:5-6). But they did not know Him! At Mount Sinai one of the most tragic events in Israel's history took place. It was there that the nation of Israel abdicated this high calling, deciding they would rather have a human mediator than know the Lord for themselves. This incident is recorded in Exodus 20:18-21:

And all the people perceived the thunder and the lightning flashes and the sound of the

trumpet and the mountain smoking; and when the people saw it, they trembled and stood at a distance.

Then they said to Moses, "Speak to us yourself and we will listen; but let not God speak to us, lest we die."

And Moses said to the people, "Do not be afraid; for God has come in order to test you, and in order that the fear of Him may remain with you, so that you may not sin."

SO THE PEOPLE STOOD AT A DISTANCE, while Moses approached the thick cloud where God was.

From this time on, the people of Israel had no desire for a personal relationship with the Lord. They wanted all the benefits of being married to Him, but they did not want Him. Sadly, this has also been the history of much of the Christian church. The church has proved willing to pay almost any price to have someone mediate her relationship with the Lord. Like Israel, the church was called to be a kingdom of priests (see Revelation 1:6). The propagation of a system that separates the priesthood from the congregation destroys the very purpose of the church.

It is an obvious, biblical position that those who are called to leadership in the church must live by standards which are not required of the whole congregation. Even so, those who are called to leadership are not called as *mediators* between God and men. "**For there is one God, and one mediator also between God and men, the man Christ Jesus**" (**I Timothy 2:5**). Whenever a man positions himself between the Lord and His people, he is usurping the position of the Lord Jesus Himself.

Jesus alone can stand between God and man. There are apostles, prophets, evangelists, pastors, teachers, elders, deacons, and other ministries that are given to the church, but they are all given **"for the equipping of the saints for the work of service, to the building up of the body of Christ; until we all attain to the unity of the faith, and of the knowledge of the Son of God, to a mature man, to the measure of the stature which belongs to the fulness of Christ"** (Ephesians 4:12-13).

No ministry is given to accomplish our own spiritual responsibilities for us. All ministries are given for the purpose of bringing the church to maturity and equipping the members to do the work of the ministry (see Ephesians 4:11-12). We are all called as ministers; we are all called as priests. When any man is called *the* minister or *the* priest, he has usurped both the Lord's and the church's authority.

Each of us is a minister and priest, though our roles will differ according to our particular gifting. This does not in any way negate the authority the Lord has established in the church. Proper ministry could not occur without this authority. Even so, the authority is of a decreasing nature, not an increasing one. As the church matures, these roles become increasingly unnecessary. The ultimate purpose of leaders should be to work themselves out of a job, just as a parent's responsibility is to prepare the child for the day he is to leave the protection of the home and enter into his unique purpose. The authority of the church is given as protection for its spiritual children and to prepare them to stand as individuals in Christ.

In Numbers 11:24-29, we see in Moses the spirit of proper ministry. The Lord had Moses gather the seventy elders to the tent of meeting so He could ordain them to share Moses' responsibility and authority in the congregation. When the Spirit came upon them, they all began to prophesy. For an undisclosed reason, two of the elders had remained in the camp, but the Spirit came upon them anyway and they prophesied. When a young man informed Moses of this, Joshua exhorted him to restrain them from prophesying. Moses replied, **"Are you jealous for my sake? Would that all the LORD's people were prophets, that the LORD would put His Spirit upon them!"** (verse 29)

Moses was not threatened by this seeming encroachment upon his own domain. He knew there was more than enough for all to do! When a leader becomes protective of his spiritual domain, he has departed from true spiritual authority. It was Moses' delight to see other leaders raised up. It was not his desire to have Israel dependent upon him, and neither should we desire others to be dependent upon us. All true ministry is devoted to the end that people would individually come to know the Lord. Jesus demonstrated this same attitude: He explained to His disciples that it would be better for them if He went away so they might receive the Spirit themselves (see John 16:7).

Commissioning to Ministry

All members of the body of Christ are called to be ministers. Everyone has a definite function which is essential to the body as a whole. But just because we have been called to a ministry does not mean we are ready for it. There may be many years between the time when our calling is given and the time when we are actually commissioned. This time between the calling and the commissioning is an essential time of preparation. If we prematurely begin to walk in our ministry before being commissioned by the Holy Spirit, we are most likely hindering the fulfillment of that ministry. The will of man can never accomplish the purposes of God. It is not by might, nor by power, nor by the most noble human intentions, but only by His Spirit that the work of God is accomplished.

Each miracle of Jesus had prophetic significance. When He turned the water into wine, His first miracle, He was demonstrating one of the most important, initial lessons we should learn as we start to follow Him. The vessels were set aside and filled with water. Water is often symbolic of the Word of God (see Ephesians 5:26). This was the period of preparation in which they were to be "filled to the brim" with His teaching. After we have received God's calling, there must be a period of time in which we are set aside and filled. It is not enough to be partially filled; we must be completely full!

It is not enough to be filled with just teaching, either. The water must be turned into wine; our knowledge must become life. Only then are we ready to be poured out. Those who are poured out too soon seldom ever become "wine" or walk in the fullness of the anointing to which they have been called. The "water" they serve is refreshing and may bless many, but with patience the finest wine will be served. Those who have waited to become wine have shaken the world!

Moses is an excellent example of the Lord's preparation. He must have suspected a call to help the Israelites when he slew an Egyptian in their defense, but it was not God's time. He fled Egypt in seeming defeat. Then he spent forty years in the wilderness as a shepherd—the most humble profession of the time—before God ordained him for His work. It has been said that Satan builds a man up so he can tear him down. The Lord tears a man down so that He can build him up! There are no shortcuts to anointed ministry. Diplomas and titles may command the respect of men, but they do not impress the Lord. Once we have tasted the wine of God, water will never satisfy.

The nature of the Lord is creative. No two people are alike and no two ministries are alike. Every prophet in the Bible was strikingly unique, as were all of the apostles. When the Lord calls us to a specific ministry, we may be somewhat patterned after another ministry, but only in a very general sense. Each of us is very different from everyone else, whether in Scripture, history, or among contemporaries. For this reason, we cannot fashion ourselves into a ministry; only the Lord can do this.

The Lord is the One who is building His church and fashioning each stone. We must allow the Lord to make us as He will. We must be willing to be very different from any others. Those who race off to fulfill their calling before the proper time inevitably become cheap imitations. Those who determine just to be *different* and have not been shaped by God are even more pitiful.

Moses Strikes the Rock

In Numbers 20:8-12, we have a sobering example of one of the greatest snares to walking in spiritual power and authority. Moses was pressured greatly by people who were complaining of not having water. The Lord commanded Moses to take his rod, a symbol of the authority the Lord had given him, and *speak* to the rock to bring forth water. Instead of speaking to the rock, Moses struck it with his rod. Water came forth in abundance, but at a grave cost. The Lord's discipline was most severe: **"But the LORD said to Moses and Aaron, 'Because you have not believed Me, to treat Me as holy in the sight of the sons of Israel, therefore you shall not bring this assembly into the Land which I have given them'"** (verse 12).

It is an awesome and sobering fact that the Lord shares His authority with His people. Used in humility and submission, authority is a powerful tool. Used presumptuously, it can cost us our inheritance in Christ. The rock was Christ. The Lord's authority (rod) was not given so that we could strike Him with it! When we begin to demand compliance, we are actually commanding the Head to obey *us*. This is dangerous ground.

The body of Christ today is frequently encouraged to search the Scriptures for desired promises, hold those Scriptures up to God, and demand fulfillment. This could be the ultimate demonstration of the pride of man! It is a faulty approach which uses God's authority and principles for self-promotion. The Lord indeed wants us to learn to use the rod—but for His purposes. When pride or self-centeredness enter into spiritual authority, we are in danger of departing from true authority. Those who **"tremble at His word"** will be His habitation (see Isaiah 66:1-2). We must treat Him as holy, or else we, like Moses, may find ourselves banned from the Promised Land.

Chapter 11
THE FEAR OF GOD VS. THE FEAR OF MAN

THE PRESSURE OF THE PEOPLE SPURRED MOSES TO USE HIS rod in a manner the Lord had not commanded. The same pressure has caused the downfall of many ministries. Humility is the fear of God, not man. **"By the fear of the LORD one keeps away from evil" (Proverbs 16:6).** "The **fear of man brings a snare" (Proverbs 29:25).** For this reason Paul declared, **"If I were still trying to please men, I would not be a bond-servant of Christ" (Galatians 1:10).** If we truly fear the Lord, we will not fear anyone else. To honor and respect the Lord is to be delivered from all fear of man.

Jesus declared to the Pharisees, **"You are those who justify yourselves in the sight of men, but God knows your hearts; for that which is highly esteemed among men is detestable in the sight of God" (Luke 16:15).** If we are compelled to seek the esteem of men, we will be found doing that which is detestable. We must determine who we are going to please—man or God. We cannot please both. For this reason Jesus cautioned, **"Woe to you when all men speak well of you, for in the same way their fathers used to treat the *false* prophets"** (Luke 6:26). Our ministry will be false to the degree that it is affected by the fear of man.

We are called to be the servants of all men, loving them and laying down our lives for their salvation, but *people are not to be our masters*. Although it is not easy to love and serve people in this way without being controlled or influenced by them, we must learn to do it. As the apostle exhorted, **"With good will render service, as to the Lord, and not to men"** (Ephesians 6:7).

Saul and David

Possibly the greatest difference between King Saul and King David was in who they wanted to please. Saul feared the people more than the Lord, but David feared the Lord more than the people. When Saul was commanded to wait until the prophet Samuel returned to make a sacrifice to the Lord, he would not wait. His attempted excuse was that **"the people were scattering from me... and that the Philistines were assembling..."** (**I Samuel 13:11**).

Anyone who has walked in leadership in the church understands this pressure. When the people begin to scatter and the enemy attacks at the same time, the compulsion to just "do something" is great—even when the Lord has told us to wait. To give into those pressures is to risk losing the anointing. When Saul succumbed to fear and people-pleasing, God's anointing for leadership left him.

The Fear of God vs. the Fear of Man

If we are to function in true spiritual authority, we must be in submission to God's authority alone. Everyone who walks in spiritual authority will have to pass this test. We must fear no one but God. If He is the One who appointed us, and if He is with us, we do not have to fear anyone but Him. Neither should we fear any circumstance if we know that God has sent us.

Compromise is a deadly enemy because it is so easily justified in our minds. When Saul was later commanded to attack and utterly destroy the Amalekites, he destroyed most of them, but kept alive the king and some of the best livestock. He justified keeping the animals, saying his intention was to offer them to the Lord. In the Scriptures, the Amalekites are a type of satanic force. During Israel's wilderness journey, the Amalekites attacked from the rear, picking off the weak and the stragglers under cover of darkness, just as Satan does. The Lord commanded that the Amalekites and all their possessions be destroyed as a type, demonstrating to all subsequent generations that there can be no compromise with Satan.

During ancient times, if one king defeated another in battle and kept him alive, he did so either to make him a slave or an ally. Saul rationalized that Agag, the king of the Amalekites, could be made an ally or a servant—which is a most dangerous assumption when we consider that Agag represented Satan himself to Israel. He also reasoned that he should keep the best of the Amalekites possessions to sacrifice to the Lord. The things of Satan cannot be used in our worship of the Lord. Samuel's rebuke of Saul is a warning to us:

And Samuel said, "Has the LORD as much delight in burnt offerings and sacrifices as in

obeying the voice of the LORD? Behold, to obey is better than sacrifice, and to heed than the fat of rams.

For rebellion is as the sin of divination, and insubordination is as iniquity and idolatry..." (I Samuel 15:22-23).

Personal sacrifice will never atone for rebellion. Many have fallen into the snare of believing good works can compensate for compromise or disobedience in other areas of their lives. This is the beginning of deception and divination (sorcery). We may think of sorcery as conjuring up spirits and weaving spells, but these are just some of the more extreme manifestations. Sorcery usually begins with the subtle attempt to manipulate God, which is one of the ultimate presumptions we can have. Paul actually named sorcery as a work of the flesh (see Galatians 5:20). Sorcery (also called witchcraft) is using any spirit or device to dominate, control, or manipulate another person or situation.

The subtle pressures we may exert on others to get our way is a form of sorcery. Saul's sacrifices to the Lord as appeasements for his lack of obedience is another example of this. Such devotion to manipulation often begins when we are children and we learn we can flatter our parents to get our way or to reduce an intended punishment. If allowed to continue, this will eventually grow into much deadlier forms of manipulation. Saul's failure to repent ultimately led to him destroying the Lord's priests and actually seeking counsel from a sorcerer.

When first confronted with his disobedience, Saul confessed, "I have sinned; I have indeed transgressed the command of the LORD and your words, *because I feared the people and listened to their voice*" (**I Samuel 15:24**). Saul confessed his sin, and understood why he had sinned, *but he did not repent.*

There is a difference between confession and repentance. Confession can actually be an attempt to manipulate, as in this case with Saul. In verse 30, the real reason for Saul's confession becomes clear: **"I have sinned; but please honor me now before the elders of *my people* and before Israel, and go back with me, that I may worship the LORD *your God*").** His confession was an attempt to get Samuel to continue to honor him before the people. Had he truly repented, he would not have been so concerned about what the people thought—he would have been concerned with what God thought. Saul's words to Samuel are quite revealing when he contrasts "*my* **people**" with "**the LORD *your* God.**" This is another symptom of the earthly-minded seed of Cain.

David was of a different spirit. Throughout the narrative of his life, we are repeatedly told that **"David inquired of the Lord"** (see I and II Samuel). Even when the Amalekites kidnapped his family and the families of his men—provoking his men to threaten stoning him—David resisted taking action before seeking the Lord. The pressure must have been incredible. In a situation that would have caused even the most faithful to doubt, it was said that **"... David strengthened himself in the LORD his God"** (**I Samuel 30:6**).

David trusted in the Lord rather than in men or circumstances. This was the solid foundation upon which the throne of David was established. It was a foundation strong enough to endure forever. Any ministry that is to endure must be built upon this same foundation.

The fear of man is a snare to any ministry. The Lord called Peter "Satan" because he set his mind on man's interests instead of God's (see Matthew 16:23). James rebuked the church with a similar warning: **"You adulteresses, do you not know that friendship with the world is hostility toward God? Therefore whoever wishes to be a friend of the world makes himself an enemy of God" (James 4:4).** We are to love the world with Christ's love, but we are not to be its friend.

Satan's Basic Strategy

Compromise has robbed the church of its power. When Moses went to Pharaoh to demand freedom for Israel, Pharaoh responded with a strategy to increase Israel's yoke of bondage. This is a parallel of the strategy Satan still uses to keep men under his control and away from the cross. As soon as Moses proclaimed liberty to Israel by the word of the Lord, Pharaoh countered by giving his men instructions to work the Israelite slaves even harder: **"Let the labor be heavier on the men, and let them work at it that they may pay no attention to false words" (Exodus 5:9).**

Pharaoh's strategy was to make the burdens on God's people heavier so they would think God's promises were **"false words."** Satan does the same to us. Just before we are about to be delivered by the power of God, he heaps extra burdens on us to make us think God's Words are false.

This strategy against Israel began to work, causing them to doubt and become discouraged. To bring

DISCOURAGEMENT is Satan's first priority. If we understand the enemy's schemes, we can combat them just as Moses did. If God gives you a promise, Satan will immediately try to make you think it is not from God by attacking you in that very area. Satan's first strategy is to make us think that God's Word is false. We must learn to expect this attack when we receive a promise from God, not allowing it to discourage us or cause us to deviate from our course.

Because Moses remained steadfast, Satan's first tactic did not work. But Satan had additional strategies. His next ploy was to duplicate the miracles of God, attempting to show that God's power was no greater than his. That would mean there really was not anything special about what God was promising, for Satan could do all the same things. This tactic was meant to bring *DISORIENTATION*.

When Moses again held his course, Pharaoh gave in a little more—but only in order to devise an even more cunning strategy. He told them, **"Go, sacrifice to your God** *within the land"* **(Exodus 8:25)**. When Satan sees that we are determined to serve the Lord, he will then try to make us think we can serve God in *his* domain. He wants us to think we can still live our lives according to the ways of the world, as long as we go to church occasionally, read our Bibles dutifully, etc. Moses was not deceived by this dangerous fallacy, and neither should we be.

After seeing the Lord's power demonstrated, Pharaoh made another proposal: **"I will let you go, that you may sacrifice to the LORD your God in the wilderness;** *only you shall not go very far away"* **(Exodus 8:28)**. Sound familiar? When one begins to break free of the world to serve the Lord, he will hear from a multitude of sources about the dangers of going too far with religion. True believers refuse to let the world dictate how far they will go with the Lord. If Satan cannot keep you in complete bondage, his next strategy is to make you compromise so he can keep you in as much bondage as possible.

This was Satan's attempt to get Israel to *LOSE HER VISION* for the Promised Land—a strategy which has been effective on many Christians. When we lose our vision, we will just wander in the wilderness, making us easy prey for recapture. The call on Israel was not just to leave Egypt, but to go to the Promised Land. We must keep our vision focused on the ultimate purpose of God or we will be distracted by a lesser purpose.

After even greater demonstrations of the Lord's power, Pharaoh proposed another compromise: **"Go, serve the LORD** [no prerequisites on how far they can go now]**; only let your flocks and your herds be detained. Even your little ones may go with you" (Exodus 10:24).** Satan's last attempt at getting us to compromise is to have us leave something behind in "Egypt," because he knows that where our treasure is, there will our hearts be also (see Matthew 6:21). He knew that if they compromised to any degree at all, he would ultimately regain dominion over them. He told them they could go as far away as they wanted, with just one condition: **"Only let your flocks and your herds be detained. Even your little ones may go with you" (Exodus 10:24).**

When Satan sees we are utterly determined to "go all the way with Jesus," he then tries to get us to leave something behind. *COMPROMISE* is spelled D-E-F-E-A-T for the people of God. We must be unrelenting in our determination to be utterly free of Satan's dominion over us or anything that is ours, responding like Moses, **"Therefore, our livestock, too, will go with us;** *not a hoof will be left behind!"* **(Exodus 10:26)**

In this scenario between Moses and Pharaoh, we have a lucid example of Satan's ancient strategy to keep God's people under his dominion. His first goal is to cause *DISCOURAGEMENT*, which leads to *DISORIENTATION*; then *LOSS OF VISION*, which leads to *COMPROMISE*; and compromise then brings *DEFEAT* to the purpose of God for His people.

Even with Pharaoh's failure to get Moses to compromise at any point, he did not give up. In the same way, we should never expect Satan to release us by his own free will. Israel was not to be freed by the dictate of Pharaoh, lest he say that *he* had let them go. Israel was only to be freed by the power of God. His power would bring destruction to the whole dominion of Pharaoh and give the treasures of Egypt into the hands of His people. We, too, must understand that we are not set free at the permission of Satan but by the power of God.

Let us make straight paths for our feet, not turning to the right or to the left, and not compromise regardless of how reasonable the proposition may seem. In this way, we will remain in the place where the power of the cross can bring us release and bring judgment upon the dominion of the evil one.

Chapter 12
THE PASSOVER

For Christ our Passover also has been sacrificed (I Corinthians 5:7).

İT WAS THE PASSOVER SACRIFICE WHICH DELIVERED ISRAEL from the power of Pharaoh so that her people would never again serve Egypt. It is the cross, of which the Passover was a prophetic type, which delivers us from the power of Satan and slavery to the corruption of the world. Realizing this, Satan rages against those who turn to the cross, just as Pharaoh raged against Israel when he saw he was losing his power over them. As the Passover did in type, the cross brings judgment upon the evils of the world and delivers all who will embrace it from the world's bondage.

Since the time of Cain and Abel, the sacrifice has been the main point of conflict between the two seeds, which represent the two natures of man—carnal and spiritual. Satan is not threatened if we embrace the doctrines or the institution of Christianity; in fact, he may well

145

encourage it. He knows that the "good" side of the Tree of Knowledge is just as deadly as the evil side, and far more deceptive.

Human goodness is an affront to the cross and is used as a compensation for it. It deludes us into thinking that if we do more "good" than evil, we will be acceptable to the Father, thereby placing us above the need for the sacrifice of His Son. Satan is happy for us to embrace anything religious as long as we do not turn to the cross. When we turn to the cross, Satan's power over us is completely broken; at that point we march out of his dominion into the glorious liberty of the Spirit.

The greatest opposition to embracing the cross and true liberty of the Spirit will come from those who are religious. This battle began with the first two brothers, Cain and Abel, and rages to this day. The cross will always be the greatest threat to the religious, and the religious will always be the greatest enemy of the cross. The demon-possessed were not the ones who persecuted Jesus; they bowed the knee and submitted to Him. The religious, moral, and conservative citizens were the ones who crucified Jesus, and these will be the ones who rise up against anyone who preaches the true message of the cross.

The greatest persecution against the true faith will always come from those who have been converted in their minds but not in their hearts. These are living by the fruit of the Tree of Knowledge instead of the fruit of the Tree of Life. Their true devotion will be to intellectual comprehension of doctrines rather than to a living relationship with God and compliance with His will.

Jesus warned, **"Not everyone who says to Me, 'Lord, Lord,' will enter the kingdom of heaven; but he who** does the will of My Father who is in heaven" **(Matthew 7:21).** We will only know true doctrine if we esteem doing His will *above* just knowing the doctrine. As Jesus explained, **"If any man is willing to do His will, he shall know of the teaching, whether it is of God, or whether I speak from Myself" (John 7:17).**

A person can desire truth for many different reasons. Some of the motivations for seeking truth are actually evil, such as pride, self-justification, or even fear. Only those who have a love for the truth will escape the deceptions of the evil day. Of course, those who love the truth do want their doctrines to be accurate, but we will only have accurate and pure doctrines if we love the God of truth more than the truths of God. It is not knowing the Book of the Lord that gives life, but knowing the Lord of the Book. We must love the Truth Himself more than we love the individual truths. If we do this, we will love those truths more than we would if we esteemed them more than we do Him. It is not a matter of having one or the other, but having both in the proper order.

A New Beginning

Now the LORD said to Moses and Aaron in the land of Egypt,

"This month shall be the beginning of months for you; it is to be the first month of the year to you" (Exodus 12:1-2).

As the Passover was to be the archetypical prophecy of the sacrifice of Jesus, it is significant to note that Moses prepared Israel for the first Passover by rotating its calendar to a **"first month."** This heralded a new beginning.

After partaking of the Passover, the children of Israel were to leave the only place they had ever known, to travel through lands they had never seen, to possess a land about which they had only dreamed. Their life would never be the same after that one, fateful day—and neither is ours.

> **Therefore if any man be in Christ, he is a new creature: old things are passed away; behold, all things are become new (II Corinthians 5:17 KJV).**

When Jesus becomes our Passover, we are born again into a new world. To Israel it was a physical change; to us it is a spiritual change. The external conditions and surroundings may remain the same, but we do not. If the externals suddenly appear different, it may be because our eyes are new! When a person is born again, he begins to see the kingdom of God (see John 3:3). This is a far more glorious deliverance. Moses led Israel out of Egypt in one day, but "Egypt" (the ways of the world) still remained in Israel. Through Christ **"the world has been crucified to me, and I to the world" (Galatians 6:14).**

Jesus takes Egypt out of the heart and replaces it with a new country—the kingdom of God. The seed of Cain, religious man, is forever seeking to make the world a better place in which to live. Christ changes men so that they might be better able to live in the world. The carnal man seeks to change men by changing the world. The spiritual man seeks to change the world by changing men.

Except for this tiny little pocket of darkness called earth, the glory of God prevails over the universe. Even though we are but a speck in the great expanse of creation, the Father made the supreme sacrifice to redeem and restore us by sending His own Son, to the overwhelming wonder of creation. But for this awesome fact, earth would register "zero" in significance compared to the expanse of God's dominion. When we begin to perceive the Lord and the dimensions of His kingdom, personal and even world problems begin to look insignificant. We can be sure that this one drop of evil in the great expanse of His creation will never overcome the oceans of His goodness. His kingdom will come! It is an irresistible force which will overshadow evil just as the sun overshadows the moon when it rises.

When man ate of the Tree of Knowledge, his attention became focused upon himself and he began to think of himself as the center of the universe. Every child born after the Fall inherited this deception. Our little problems and ambitions completely dominate our minds until we are converted. Then, as we begin to see the kingdom of God, our perspective is changed.

The more clearly we see Him sitting on His throne, the less we notice the problems and cares of the world. Not that we are insensitive to human needs—we simply realize that He is vastly bigger than any problem and more wonderful than any human solution! As we see Him with new eyes, we find a peace that is beyond comprehension. The world may not be one bit different, but we are.

Walking in Truth

Walking in truth is walking with God. As our vision of His kingdom is clarified, the things of earth do grow dim. The things that are invisible to the natural man become more real to us than things that are seen. To those who do not see in the Spirit, this sounds absurd. The apostle Paul explained it well:

149

But a natural man does not accept the things of the Spirit of God; for they are foolishness to him, and he cannot understand them, because they are spiritually appraised.

But he who is spiritual appraises all things [accurately], yet he himself is appraised by no man (I Corinthians 2:14-15).

If we were to wake up tomorrow and see Jesus standing beside our bed, the day at the office would probably be quite different! How would the day change if He were to visibly accompany us throughout the day? To those born of the Spirit, "the eyes of the heart" see more clearly than the natural eyes, and they always behold the Lord. Because the Lord lives in us, He is with us wherever we go. When we behold Him in the power of His resurrection—as the King over all rulers, powers, and authorities—we will also have the faith to approach any person or circumstance with great boldness.

When Stephen was martyred, he was not distracted even by the stones which were killing him. He was looking at Jesus! The apostle Paul, who was yet unconverted, witnessed the reality of Stephen's vision as he was being stoned. The Lord was even then preparing His chosen vessel to carry His name before the Gentiles, kings, and the sons of Israel. The seed planted in Paul's heart when he saw Stephen's ability to see the invisible was to bear much fruit. Years later Paul wrote these penetrating verses urging the Ephesian Christians to see into the unseen realm:

I pray that the eyes of your heart may be enlightened, so that you may know what is the

hope of His calling, what are the riches of the glory of His inheritance in the saints,

and what is the surpassing greatness of His power toward us who believe. These are in accordance with the working of the strength of His might

which He brought about in Christ, when He raised Him from the dead, and seated Him at His right hand in the heavenly places,

far above all rule and authority and power and dominion, and every name that is named, not only in this age, but also in the one to come.

And He put all things in subjection under His feet, and gave Him as head over all things to the church,

which is His body, the fulness of Him who fills all in all (Ephesians 1:18-23).

When Paul perceived Jesus on His throne, he saw all things subjected to Him. Jesus is still on the throne. *All* dominion has been given to Him, and nothing can happen that He does not allow. It is impossible for Satan to sneak in a blow when Jesus is not looking. When the eyes of our hearts are opened to see this, it is difficult to give much credence to the cares of the world.

Elisha was another who had this heavenly vision. When confronted by an entire army, he sat peacefully on the side of a hill, much to his servant's dismay. When Elisha prayed for the servant's eyes to be opened, the servant was then able to understand the reason for

Elisha's confidence: the angels standing for them outnumbered the enemy (see II Kings 6:8-23). In any circumstance, those with a heavenly perspective know that those who are with us greatly outnumber those who are against us.

Walking in the Spirit

To walk in the Spirit is to see with His eyes, hear with His ears, and understand with His heart. As we do this, the earth, with all of its problems and its glories, begins to appear as small as it really is. After we have beheld the glory and authority of Jesus, kings and presidents are no more impressive than the destitute. Once we have seen the Lord, all earthly pomp and position appear ludicrous, and even the worst international crisis is hardly cause for concern. The King is on His throne, and He will never lose control.

When Isaiah saw the Lord sitting on His throne, there were seraphim with Him who called out to one another, **"Holy, Holy, Holy, is the LORD of hosts,** *the whole earth is full of His glory"* **(Isaiah 6:3).** With all of the wars, conflicts, disasters, diseases, and confusion, how can the seraphim say that the whole earth is full of His glory? They are able to say it because they dwell in the presence of the Lord.

As we begin to dwell in His presence, we, too, will see the whole earth as being full of His glory, regardless of the circumstances. We see the reality of what is taking place on earth, but we also see the greater reality of God's plan and power. We are citizens of the new creation, not the old, and we must see from the perspective of the new.

Now we might ask why we have this continual battle with our old nature if we are new creatures. We would not have this battle if we kept our eyes on Jesus. It is when we, like Peter, take our eyes off Him and focus on the tossing waves of the world and the flesh that we begin to sink. Paul explained this to the Romans:

> **For I know that nothing good dwells in me, that is, in my flesh; for the wishing is present in me, but the doing of the good is not.**

> **For the good that I wish, I do not do; but I practice the very evil that I do not wish.**

> **But if I am doing the very thing I do not wish, I am no longer the one doing it, but sin which dwells in me.**

> **I find then the principle that evil is present in me, the one who wishes to do good.**

> **For I joyfully concur with the law of God in the inner man,**

> **but I see a different law in the members of my body, waging war against the law of my mind, and making me a prisoner of the law of sin which is in my members.**

> **Wretched man that I am! Who will set me free from the body of this death?**

> **Thanks be to God through Christ Jesus our Lord! (Romans 7:18-25)**

Without Christ, there is no good thing in us. No matter how many times we look at ourselves, we will find the same thing—evil. But in Christ we no longer have to live by our sinful nature! He has given us His Life, His Spirit! When He said, **"It is finished" (John 19:30)**, He meant it. He is the finished work of God; He is the finished work the Father seeks to accomplish in us.

Maturity is not accomplished by striving to reach a certain level of spirituality—maturity is simply abiding in Him Who is the finished work of God. Jesus *is* our wisdom, righteousness, sanctification, and redemption (see I Corinthians 1:30). Jesus is everything we are called to be; we can only fulfill our calling by abiding in Him.

We will never become the new creation simply by setting spiritual goals and attaining them. We can only attain true spirituality by abiding in the One who *is* the work of God. Jesus is the Alpha and Omega, the Beginning and the End of all things. Jesus is called **"the first-born of all creation" (Colossians 1:15)**. Jesus is the whole Purpose of God. As stated, and it is a statement worthy of repeating—everything that the Father loved and esteemed, He brought forth in His Son. Everything was created *by* Him, and *for* Him, and *in* Him all things hold together (see Colossians 1:16-17). The whole creation was *for* the Son. All things are to be summed up in Him (see Ephesians 1:10). We accomplish the whole purpose of God in our life when we have our whole being summed up in Him by simply abiding.

> **See to it that no one takes you captive through philosophy and empty deception, according to the tradition of men, according to the elementary principles of the world, rather than according to Christ.**

> "For in Him all the fulness of Deity dwells in bodily form,
>
> and in Him you have been made complete..." (Colossians 2:8-10).

If we do not stay focused on the ultimate purpose of God—that all things are to be summed up in Christ—we will be in danger of continually being distracted by the lesser purposes of God, or even worse, by the interests of the world.

Changing the Heart

We can, in our own strength, change our outward behavior to some degree, but only the Lord can change our hearts. We cannot even judge the thoughts and intentions of our hearts accurately, for **"the heart is more deceitful than all else and is desperately sick; who can understand it?" (Jeremiah 17:9)**. We may have pretty good motives one day and terrible ones the next. If we only do things when our motives are right, we will easily be foiled by Satan or deceived by our own hearts, even while we may have the best of intentions. If we allow our motives to control us, we will be in perpetual confusion. Our lives must be determined by the will of God, not our motives. Paul explained this to the Corinthians:

> But to me it is a very small thing that I should be examined by you, or by any human court; in fact, I do not even examine myself.
>
> For I am conscious of nothing against myself, yet I am not by this acquitted; but the one who examines me is the Lord (I Corinthians 4:3-4).

There Were Two Trees in the Garden

This does not mean that we ignore our problems, but we must depend upon the Lord's Word to divide between soul and spirit. Even though we are encouraged to "judge ourselves" so that we will not be judged (see I Corinthians 11:31), this must be done by the Spirit. Our judgment of ourselves will be distorted if it is not done by the Spirit. Our hearts are deceitful and often this results even more in self-deception than in deceiving others. We must depend on the Lord to change us if the change is to be real. We are changed as we behold His glory, not our own failings (see II Corinthians 3:18).

But we must not be presumptuous. Although intro-spection is not our solution, we do not have license to follow evil motives or pursue our own ends. Through Jesus, God **"condemned sin in the flesh" (Romans 8:3).** Depicting God's grace as continual forgiveness for continual sin is a dangerous, false doctrine. When we abuse His grace and live after the flesh, we have departed from authentic grace.

He promised that we will never be tempted beyond what we are able to endure (see I Corinthians 10:13). The grace the Lord has given us is the *power* to walk by His Spirit. As Peter stated, **"seeing that His divine power has granted** [past tense] **to us** *everything* **pertaining to life and godliness** [Godlikeness]**, through the true knowledge of Him..." (II Peter 1:3).**

When we give in to the flesh, it is not because we do not have the strength to resist—we are simply giving in to sin! It is like training for a marathon. When the runner thinks he cannot go another step, he will find that he can go a great deal farther if he will only relax. His endurance increases from that point. When we get to the place where we do not think we can stand the temptation any longer, victory will come if we rest in Him who has conquered all sin. By abiding in Him we will find strength to endure far past the point at which we usually give up. It is at the very point where we cannot stand it any longer that His strength takes over.

> **"My grace is sufficient for you, for power is perfected in weakness" (II Corinthians 12:9).**

> **Therefore, do not throw away your confidence, which has a great reward.**

> **For you have need of endurance, so that when you have done the will of God, you may receive what was promised.**

> **For yet in a very little while, He who is coming will come, and will not delay.**

> **But My righteous one shall live by faith; and if he shrinks back, My soul has no pleasure in him.**

> **But we are not of those who shrink back to destruction, but of those who have faith to the preserving of the soul (Hebrews 10:35-39).**

The athlete's endurance does not increase until he reaches the previous limit of his endurance and overtakes it. The same is true of our spiritual endurance. We can testify with Paul, **"I can do all things through Him who strengthens me" (Philippians 4:13).** In Christ we can never say "cannot" to what He has called us to do. We can say we that we "will not" or "did not," but we can never say that we "cannot." He has given us *His* strength.

And in Him you were also circumcised with a circumcision made without hands, in the removal of the body of the flesh by the circumcision of Christ (Colossians 2:11).

There is therefore now no condemnation for those who are in Christ Jesus.

For the law of the Spirit of life in Christ Jesus has set you free from the law of sin and of death.

For what the Law could not do, weak as it was through the flesh, God did: sending His own Son in the likeness of sinful flesh and as an offering for sin, He condemned sin in the flesh,

in order that the requirement of the Law might be fulfilled in us, who do not walk according to the flesh, but according to the Spirit (Romans 8:1-4).

The Lord is not just trying to change us; He is trying to *kill* us! The ultimate high calling of God is attained when we can say with the apostle, "**I have been crucified with Christ; and it is no longer I who live, but Christ lives in me; and the life which I now live in the flesh I live by faith in the Son of God, who loved me, and delivered Himself up for me**" (Galatians 2:20).

John the Baptist was a wonderful type of true, spiritual ministry. His whole purpose and devotion was to prepare the way for Jesus, to point to Him, and then to decrease as He increased. John did not say that he would decrease *so that* Jesus could increase. He simply stated,

"**He must increase, but I must decrease**" (John 3:30). If we try to decrease *so* Jesus can increase, we are still pursuing a self-righteousness by which we try to dictate His increase.

Again, it is as we see Him and His glory that we are changed into His image (see II Corinthians 3:18). Only then will there be a true decrease of our own self-life. To presume that we can crucify our own flesh is vanity. If we were somehow able to crucify ourselves, all that we would have left is self-righteousness. Instead of crucifying ourselves, we are crucified "**with Christ.**"

The new birth is possibly the greatest demonstration of the love and grace of God. We have all sinned and are worthy of eternal destruction. But the Father so loved us that He sent His own Son to be a propitiation for our sins, allowing us to start all over again. We exchange our body of death for eternal life as the Lord's own children. No genius of fantasy or fiction could have ever dreamed a more wonderful story. How could we who have partaken of such glory not "**do all things for the sake of the gospel?**" (**I Corinthians 9:23**)

> *For the love of Christ controls us*, **having concluded this, that one died for all, therefore all died;**

> **and He died for all,** *that they who live should no longer live for themselves, but for Him* **who died and rose again on their behalf.**

> **Therefore from now on we recognize no man according to the flesh; even though we have known Christ according to the flesh, yet now we know Him thus no longer.**

Therefore if any man is in Christ, he is a new creature; the old things passed away; behold, new things have come.

Now all these things are from God, who reconciled us to Himself through Christ, and gave us the ministry of reconciliation,

namely, that God was in Christ reconciling the world to Himself, not counting their trespasses against them, and He has committed to us the word of reconciliation.

Therefore, we are ambassadors for Christ, as though God were entreating through us; we beg you on behalf of Christ, be reconciled to God.

He made Him who knew no sin to be sin on our behalf, that we might become the righteousness of God in Him (II Corinthians 5:14-21).

Chapter 13
TAKING THE LAMB INTO THE HOUSE

Speak to all the congregation of Israel, saying, "On the tenth of this month they are each one to take a lamb for themselves, according to their fathers' households, a lamb for each household.

And you shall keep it until the fourteenth day of the same month..." (Exodus 12:3,6).

THE PURPOSE OF TAKING THE LAMB INTO THE HOUSE FIVE days before the sacrifice was to carefully examine it for flaws. This was a prophecy that Jesus, the true Passover Lamb, would enter Jerusalem five days before His crucifixion. He did this, of course, perfectly fulfilling the prophecy. While He was entering the city, the ritual Passover lambs were themselves being taken into the houses.

As these lambs were being examined for disqualifying flaws, the scribes, Pharisees, and Sadducees were challenging Jesus trying to find a flaw in Him. Despite their intense scrutiny, no blemish was found. He was the acceptable sacrifice for God's Passover. The rulers finally resigned themselves to hiring false witnesses against Him.

In John 19:42, we note that Jesus was slain on the Jewish Day of Preparation. On this day all the Passover lambs were slain to prepare for the feast. As Jesus was nailed to the cross, knives were being put to the throats of sacrificial lambs throughout Israel. The fulfillment of the type was taking place right in their midst.

Jesus alone is the Lamb who is without blemish. Our acceptance by the Father was determined at the cross and is therefore not based on how well we are doing on any particular day. Our ability to come boldly before the throne of grace must never be measured by how good or bad we have been, but by the blood of Jesus. Coming on any other basis is an affront to the sacrifice He made for us on the cross. The cross alone has gained our approval from God.

True ministry, then, is not done in order to gain God's approval; it comes from a position of *having* His approval, because of the cross. Our obedience comes from being in Him, not in order to achieve a position. We love Him because He first loved us. We now labor because we love Him, and we long to see Him receive the reward of His sacrifice. There is a vast difference between trying to please God because we love Him and trying to please Him in order to gain His acceptance. The former is worship; the latter is still the self-seeking pursuit of self-righteousness.

Our failure to understand this aspect of the Passover may well explain why there is such a superficial nature to many modern conversions. Major international evangelists confess that less than 5 percent of those who make a decision in their crusades go on to walk with the Lord. Could it be there is something lacking in the gospel we preach? Could it be that instead of trying to get such hasty "decisions" we would serve lost people better if, like Israel, we encouraged them to take the Lamb into their "houses" for a few days before they embrace the sacrifice? Would the decisions not be more real if people were encouraged to first examine Jesus thoroughly so they would know for themselves that there is no flaw in Him?

Sometimes a person is ready to make a decision to be reborn immediately. But generally, our modern evangelistic methods are not bearing fruit that remains. In the parable of the sower, the Lord said, **"When anyone hears the word of the kingdom, and does not understand it, the evil one comes and snatches away what has been sown in his heart..."** (Matthew 13:19). Likewise, He said, **"and the one on whom seed was sown on the good ground, this is the man *who hears the word and understands it...*"** (verse 23).

There are times when we need to heed the biblical exhortation to not lean on our own understanding (see Proverbs 3:5), but not at conversion. Those who make a commitment because of hype, emotional stimulation, or even at the prompting of anointed preaching are in danger of having the seed snatched away if they do not understand it. If one is inclined to trust an issue as significant as eternal life to something he does not understand, is it even possible that he has truly believed in his heart?

As precious as redemption, salvation, and the purposes of God are, one who has truly believed in his heart will be compelled to sink his roots as deep as possible into these matters. True faith is not blind; it is illumination in the most profound sense. True faith has nothing to fear from examination; it has everything to gain. There is a difference between believing in the mind and believing in the heart; they are not mutually exclusive.

If we are truly examining Jesus, not just intellectual concepts, the more closely we look at Him the more our hearts will be stirred to believe. Even Napoleon, after reading the gospel of John, stated that if Jesus was not the Son of God, then the one who wrote that gospel was! He realized that the story he was reading was far beyond any human invention. Those who truly examine Him will always find the same thing. Those who do not truly examine Him before accepting Him will be much more subject to future doubts, and therefore much more prone to fall away.

Who Do You Say that He Is?

There was a time when Jesus asked His disciples who men said that He was. They answered, **"Some say John the Baptist; and others, Elijah; but still others, Jeremiah, or one of the prophets" (Matthew 16:14).** He then challenged them with the question, **"But who do *you* say that I am?" (verse 15).** If they were to be true disciples, they could not be following Him because of who others said He was. The same is true with us. It is not who our pastor says Jesus is, or our favorite author, teacher, or televangelist. Sooner or later His finger will be pointed right in our own chest—"Who do *you* say that the Son of Man is?" We cannot be converted to another man's Jesus; He has got to be *our* Jesus.

When Peter answered that Jesus was the Christ, the Son of God, the Lord replied, **"Blessed are you, Simon Barjona, because flesh and blood did not reveal this to you, but My Father who is in heaven" (verse 17).** Peter was obviously not just moved by what others thought of Jesus; he was open to receive his own revelation. Like Peter, when we are open to receiving our own revelation from the Father, we are building upon a Rock that the gates of hell cannot prevail against. A parrot can learn to say the right things and do the right things, but its heart is not involved. If our understanding is simply the parroting of another, it is not true understanding, it is not in our hearts, and it will never stand the test which surely comes upon every seed that is planted.

This is not meant to be an attack upon any particular evangelist's methods. Like Paul, we should rejoice that Jesus is being preached even if the results are not perfect. Even if just one percent are converted, this is still a great many who may not have been reached had these men not been out there laboring. But there is wisdom in the biblical pattern of having those who would partake of the Passover sacrifice examine the Lamb thoroughly before doing so. We will not lose any true converts by doing this; perhaps we will gain many.

Chapter 14
HE WAS CRUCIFIED BY US

The whole assembly of the congregation of Israel is to kill it [the lamb] at twilight (Exodus 12:6).

And *all the people* answered and said, "His blood be on us and on our children" (Matthew 27:25).

As PROPHESIED, IT WAS THE WHOLE CONGREGATION OF Israel that delivered Jesus to be crucified. Yet it was not just Israel that crucified Him; it was the carnal nature that is within us all. Had the Lord chosen to send His Son to any other nation, there would have been the same result. Even Plato perceived that a truly righteous man would be despised by all men and would eventually be impaled, which was the Greek equivalent of crucifixion.

True Christians have always been persecuted and are still persecuted in almost every nation of the world. The Lord Himself declared, "to the extent that you did it to

one of these brothers of Mine, even the least of them,
you did it to Me" (Matthew 25:40). Jesus has completely
identified Himself with those for whom He died. If we
have ever persecuted, slandered, or brought injury upon
any of His, we have done it to the Lord Himself. If we
have betrayed a congregation, a minister, or a brother—
even one who is the least, even one who is in doctrinal
error or has other problems—we have betrayed the Lord
Himself.

Criticizing God

We must stop casting stones at others who fall short
of God's glory, for we have also fallen. When we judge
another servant or congregation of the Lord, we are in
fact judging Him. When we judge one of God's children,
we are in effect saying, His workmanship does not meet
up to our standards—we could do it better!

When the people rose up against Moses, his reply was,
they were not rebelling against him but against God (see
Exodus 16:8). Moses did not mean by this that he was
perfect or everything he did was perfect. But he saw that
since God had appointed him as the leader, if they rebelled
against him they were rebelling against God's provision.

The same may be true of our tendency to judge leaders
or even circumstances. If we are critical of a person or of a
particular circumstance the Lord has us in, we are in effect
saying we do not think the Lord knows what He is doing
in ordering our life. We are not just judging the circumstance, we are judging God. The same may be true if we
are judging our spouses, families, or superiors. How can

we trust the Lord with our eternal salvation if we cannot trust Him in the everyday matters of life?

Of course, there are cases where we are in the wrong job or other circumstances because we failed to seek the Lord and follow His guidance, but that still does not give us the right to rebel. In such cases we should repent and pray for change, not being critical of our situations but of our own foolishness.

There has been a long conflict in the church over the doctrines of God's sovereignty and man's free will. The problem is not that these two doctrines are in conflict; they only seem to be so when we look at them from an earthly, human perspective. They are both true. God is completely sovereign, but He has also given us free will.

That is why He put the Tree of Knowledge in the Garden. There could be no true obedience from the heart unless there was the freedom to disobey. There could be no true worship without the freedom *not* to worship. Otherwise the Lord would have done much better to have just created computers and programmed millions of them to worship Him. But would anyone appreciate such worship, much less our God?

In His sovereignty, God has given us free will, and we must make the choice to follow Him. We cannot blame all our circumstances on Him, since most of our problems are the result of our wrong choices— choices made without seeking Him. Either way, there is never a justification for grumbling and complaining. Grumbling and complaining caused the first generation who left Egypt to die in the wilderness, and will surely keep us from receiving God's provision as well (see I Corinthians 10:10; Philippians 2:14-15).

Like Israel, if we do not face our circumstances with faith, regardless of how we got into them, we will go around the same mountain of trial over and over until we perish. Only when we begin to believe God will we be able to progress on our journey.

Possibly the greatest reason for the church's lack of light, power, and a closer relationship with the Lord is her critical spirit. God directly addressed this through the prophet Isaiah:

> **Then your light will break out like the dawn, and your recovery will speedily spring forth; and your righteousness will go before you; the glory of the LORD will be your rear guard.**
>
> **Then you will call, and the LORD will answer; you will cry, and He will say, "Here I am."** *IF you remove the yoke from your midst, the pointing of the finger, and speaking wickedness...* **(Isaiah 58:8-9).**

The Lord here promises light, restoration, righteousness, the glory of the Lord, and answered prayer—if we remove the yoke of the critical spirit (pointing the finger and speaking wickedness). As if we needed even more motivation than this to repent of this evil, Jesus gave it to us:

> **Do not judge lest you be judged.**
>
> **For in the way you judge, you will be judged; and by your standard of measure, it will be measured to you (Matthew 7:1-2).**

We have seen this so often fulfilled. Those who set themselves up as judges to criticize others end up becoming stumbling blocks, doing more damage to the church in the name of truth than many do with error, and receiving upon themselves a much more severe judgment. The Lord reserved His most serious warning for those who would be stumbling blocks:

> **It is inevitable that stumbling blocks should come, but woe to him through whom they come!**

> **It would be better for him if a millstone were hung around his neck and he were thrown into the sea, than that he should cause one of these little ones to stumble (Luke 17:1-2).**

Jude was likewise most severe when explaining the judgment reserved for those he called "faultfinders":

> **But these men revile the things which they do not understand; and the things which they know by instinct, like unreasoning animals, by these things they are destroyed.**

> **Woe to them! For they have gone the way of Cain, and for pay they have rushed headlong into the error of Balaam, and perished in the rebellion of Korah.**

> **These men are those who are hidden reefs in your love feasts when they feast with you without fear, caring for themselves; clouds without water, carried along by winds; autumn trees without fruit, doubly dead, uprooted;**

wild waves of the sea, casting up their own shame like foam; wandering stars, for whom the black darkness has been reserved forever.

And about these also Enoch, in the seventh generation from Adam, prophesied, saying, "Behold, the Lord came with many thousands of His holy ones,

to execute judgment upon all, and to convict all the ungodly of all their ungodly deeds which they have done in an ungodly way, and of all the harsh things which ungodly sinners have spoken against Him."

These are grumblers, finding fault, following after their own lusts; they speak arrogantly, flattering people for the sake of gaining an advantage.

But you, beloved, ought to remember the words that were spoken beforehand by the apostles of our Lord Jesus Christ,

that they were saying to you, "In the last time there shall be mockers, following after their own ungodly lusts."

These are the ones who cause divisions, worldly-minded, devoid of the Spirit.

But you, beloved, building yourselves up on your most holy faith; praying in the Holy Spirit;

keep yourselves in the love of God, waiting anxiously for the mercy of our Lord Jesus Christ to eternal life (Jude 10-21).

Righteous Judgments

In addressing the Corinthian problem of immorality, Paul asked, **"Do you not judge those who are within the church?" (I Corinthians 5:12)** Those in leadership do have the authority and the responsibility to judge those who are within the church, but there is a certain biblical pattern which must be followed. This proper form of judgment can almost always be distinguished from that which comes from stumbling blocks, since it complies with the biblical wisdom for judging within the church. First, we are commanded to go alone to the person we believe is in sin or error. If the person does not repent, we are then to take another with us to entreat him further. Only if the person fails to repent after this is permission given to bring the issue before the church (see Matthew 18:15-17).

The Lord's command as to the manner in which we are to reprove those who are in error was given immediately following His exhortation concerning stumbling blocks. Those who go public with their accusations without complying with this mandate have almost certainly placed themselves in jeopardy of being stumbling blocks, regardless of how accurate their judgment is. This is a much more serious transgression than most of the other sins for which leaders would have to confront members of the church. Although there are appointed leaders in the church who must handle such matters, they must be extremely careful. We would have to be the greatest of fools to presume to do this without having been clearly appointed to it by the Lord.

Even if we comply with biblical procedures for confronting sin, we can still be in error if we do it in the wrong spirit, as Paul warned the Galatians:

> **Brethren, even if a man is caught in *any* trespass, you who are spiritual, *restore* such a one in a spirit of gentleness; each one looking to yourself, lest you too be tempted (Galatians 6:1).**

Note that this command is to **"restore"** a brother who is caught in **"*any* trespass."** Restoration implies much more than just forgiving. We should reject the ministry of anyone who casts judgments on others without an obvious devotion to seeing the ones they are questioning restored. Those who are not following the biblical commands of the Lord in Matthew 18, and who do not display a clear desire to further the restoration of those who are in error, are the faultfinders whom Jude wrote about. We are commanded not only to remove such from our midst, but to **"mark them which cause divisions and offences contrary to the doctrine which ye have learned; and avoid them" (Romans 16:17 KJV).**

There is a reason why those who go public with their judgment of others will usually end up falling themselves and doing so publicly. The repercussions for speaking in a critical spirit about a brother is bad in this life, but it will be even more terrible when we stand before the Lord's judgment seat. Those who measure out judgment will have it measured back to them in the same measure. Those who show mercy will receive mercy; those who give grace will receive the same. Since we are all in desperate need of mercy and grace, let us be devoted to likewise being vessels for them.

> **"But I say to you that everyone who is angry with his brother shall be guilty before the court; and whoever shall say to his brother, "Raca," shall be guilty before the supreme court; and whoever shall say, 'Raca,' shall be guilty enough to go into the fiery hell.**
>
> **"If therefore you are presenting your offering at the altar, and there remember that your brother has something against you,**
>
> **"leave your offering there before the altar, and go your way; first be reconciled to your brother, and then come and present your offering" (Matthew 5:22-24).**

Some have misconstrued this text as describing the need to confront someone we have something against (see Matthew 18:15), but that is not what it is saying. While we are commanded to *forgive* those who have wronged us, we are asked to *go and make right* what someone may have *against us*. This requires us to show mercy *without expecting or requiring it from others*. The response people make to our efforts at reconciliation is between them and the Lord; we are to be concerned only with the correctness of our own actions and attitudes.

This may seem unfair, and indeed, the Lord does not mean for it to be fair. If we want what is fair, we have all sinned and are worthy of death! Every chance we have to forgive and show mercy or grace is a great opportunity to receive more mercy and grace from the Lord. Yet when we forgive someone or show them mercy, let us do it secretly before the Father that He may reward us. When we do acts of kindness in such a way that we gain recognition, we have already received our reward by that recognition.

A wonderful story is told about a South Pacific culture where it was the custom of men to trade cows for a wife. A father could expect to receive two cows for an average daughter. An above-average girl would usually bring her father three cows. Only a rare beauty would ever bring four cows. One father had a daughter so homely that he was hoping to receive even one cow for her. There was also a man on the island who was considered their most astute trader. To everyone's astonishment, this man came and offered eight cows for the father's homely daughter! Everyone thought the wise trader had lost his mind, but it was not long before this homely girl was transformed into the most beautiful and gracious woman in the land. She had started to think of herself as "an eight-cow woman," and she became one!

We determine the value of a commodity by what someone is willing to pay for it. With what were we bought? What price was paid for our wife, husband, child, parent, friend, or boss? The most precious commodity in all of creation was paid for them—the blood of the Son of God. We must begin knowing one another after the Spirit and seeing each other as God sees us. When we do, this we will begin to see as dramatic a change in some as there was in the homely young girl from the South Pacific.

We must stop crucifying the Lord again in each other. Instead, we need to start esteeming the Lord and His workmanship in each one, giving the value to one another which He gave. Few things will work to the edification of the whole body of Christ so much as our starting to know each other after the Spirit instead of after the flesh. Let us pray to only see with His eyes, hear with His ears, and understand with His heart. Then we will be the most astute and wise men and women in the land. Unrighteous judgment kills, but mercy gives life. That is why it is written:

> **So speak and so act, as those who are to be judged by the law of liberty.**
>
> **For judgment will be merciless to one who has shown no mercy; mercy triumphs over judgment (James 2:12-13).**

Because the Word is also clear that we will reap what we sow (see Galatians 6:7), if we want to receive grace we need to sow it every chance we get. If we want to receive mercy, we need to extend it every chance we get. We should be looking for every opportunity to forgive people, show them mercy, and give them grace.

Becoming God's Spokesman

> **Therefore, thus says the LORD, "If you return, then I will restore you—before Me you will stand; *And if you extract the precious from the worthless, you will become My spokesman*" (Jeremiah 15:19).**

When we start to see the precious in that which appears worthless and begin speaking to it, drawing it out of one another, we will start to become the prophetic people we must be in order to accomplish the mandate of God for this hour. Let us stop crucifying Christ again when He comes in even the least of His little ones. Let us start recognizing Him, honoring Him, and calling Him forth in one another.

The Pharisees in the first century expected to see the Messiah come on His white horse, conquering and reigning. Today when many Christians look for Christ in His people they are expecting the same glory and victory. This is truly Jesus' state in heaven, but if we want to see Him in His people, we sometimes have to have the heart of Simeon and Anna. They were able to see in a mere infant the salvation of the whole world.

We are sometimes so busy looking for the fruit that we fail to see the seed that is to become the fruit. Let us be discerning enough not to miss Him in whatever form He appears. True wise men will worship Him even in His infancy. True apostles are yet in labor that Christ might be formed in His people. True prophets are always looking for the One they are called to point to and acknowledge, preparing His way and making it straight.

Chapter 15
THE LIFE IS IN THE BLOOD

> **Moreover, they shall take some of the blood and put it on the two door posts and on the lintel of the houses in which they eat it (Exodus 12:7).**

THE ANGEL OF DEATH COULD NOT TOUCH THE HOUSES THAT had the lamb's blood applied to them. Without the blood, they would have been doomed to the same judgment that came upon Egypt. It is by the application of the blood of Jesus to our lives that we are freed from God's judgment against the world and its sin, the wages of that sin being death. Nothing more or less will save us.

It would not have done Israel any good to sacrifice the Passover lamb *unless they also applied its blood to their houses.* Likewise, it will not benefit us just to realize that a propitiation for our sins was needed or even to know that Jesus made the propitiation—*unless His blood is applied to our lives.* To know facts without applying them accomplishes nothing. Even the demons know and believe the doctrine of salvation. It is not knowing in our minds, but believing in our hearts which brings salvation (see Romans 10:9-10).

The Lord explained through Moses that **"the life of the flesh is in the blood" (Leviticus 17:11).** It is only by the application of the life of Jesus to our lives that we are saved: **"We were reconciled to God through the death of His Son, much more, having been reconciled, WE SHALL BE SAVED BY HIS LIFE" (Romans 5:10).** The simple recognition of historic facts or understanding of spiritual principles does not accomplish this; our lives must be infused with His life.

Because knowledge has so often been substituted for life, many have been made to feel comfortable in a spiritual condition where they remain lost. Just having knowledge does not mean it has been applied. One can know all about electrical theory, but it is of no help if he does not turn on the light switch.

The Increase of Knowledge

There has been a great increase of knowledge during these last days, including spiritual knowledge. We are going to need every bit of it to accomplish the mandate the Lord has given us for this day. But the substitution of knowledge for life has led to much of the shallowness and lack of power in the church today. Knowledge only puffs up unless it leads to transformation and life. The Way is not a formula, but a Person. Truth is not just the assimilation and comprehension of spiritual facts, but a Person. And unless we have come to know Jesus as our Life, we do not really know the Way or the Truth either.

The Life Is In the Blood

The miracles performed by the Lord were not done just to impress us with His power; they were meant to convey a message. His first miracle is the first one we need to understand. Through it He was showing His newly gathered disciples the initial work to be done in them. At the wedding in Cana, the Lord ordered the vessels set aside. These vessels were typical of the disciples. He then had them filled with water, which is typical of the Word of God. The water was then turned into wine, testifying of the fact that the Word would be changed into Spirit and Life.

Once we have tasted this wine we will never again be satisfied with mere water. Not only will we yearn for the Lord to fill us to the brim with water, we will patiently wait to serve that water to others until He has turned it into the finest wine. This is what Paul meant when he said, **"when He who had set me apart, even from my mother's womb, and called me through His grace, was pleased to reveal His Son in me** [not just to him]**, that I might preach..."** **(Galatians 1:15-16).**

Paul explained how the blood was applied to his life when he declared, **"*I have been* [past tense] crucified with Christ; and it is no longer I who live, but Christ lives in me..."** **(Galatians 2:20).** Salvation is more than just forgiveness for sinful actions; it is deliverance from the indwelling evil that causes those actions! The crucifixion of Jesus accomplished an exchange for us— our body of death for His resurrection life. It is true that we must die to our lives, interests, and will to partake of Him, but no creature in all of creation will ever make a more profitable transaction.

Communion

> And they shall eat the flesh that same
> night, roasted with fire, and they shall eat it
> with unleavened bread and bitter herbs
> (Exodus 12:8).

> Jesus therefore said to them, "Truly, truly,
> I say to you, unless You eat the flesh of the Son
> of Man and drink His blood, you have no life
> in yourselves.

> "He who eats My flesh and drinks My
> blood has eternal life, and I will raise him up
> on the last day.

> "For My flesh is true food, and My
> blood is true drink. He who eats My flesh and
> drinks My blood abides in Me, and I in him.

> "As the living Father sent Me, and I live
> because of the Father, so he who eats Me, he
> also shall live because of Me" (John 6:53-57).

"We are what we eat" is a common axiom in relation
to natural foods, but it is just as true in relation to our
spiritual food. If we are partaking of the Lord Jesus, the
Tree of Life, we will become that Life. Jesus did not
say "he who has eaten My flesh," but "**he who** *eats*" or
he who continues to eat. This speaks of our need to
continually partake of Him and abide in Him. He is the
true Manna from heaven (see John 6:58). Just as Israel
had to gather fresh manna each day because it would spoil
if stored, we, too, must seek Him afresh each day. We
cannot be sustained on day-old revelation. We cannot set

aside one day a week to be spiritual and expect to abide in Him the rest of the week. He must be new to us every morning.

When the Lord referred to the eating of His flesh and drinking of His blood, of course He was not talking of His physical flesh and blood but of what they symbolically represented—His life and His body, the church (we are bone of His bone and flesh of His flesh). Perplexed by what He said, most of those who heard this departed from Him (see John 6:66). Although confused leaders of the church later reduced this truth to the ritual of the Eucharist, what Jesus referred to is a *reality*, not just a ritual.

To partake of the ritual is not equivalent to partaking of Him. The ritual of the Lord's Supper was given as a reminder, not a substitute. When this ritual usurped the reality, the very life of the Lord was removed from the church, and she then plunged into the Dark Ages—an appropriate title for the spiritual depravity of those times.

The apostle Paul explained the meaning of this rite to the Corinthians: **"The cup of blessing which we bless, is it not the communion of the blood of Christ? The bread which we break, is it not the communion of the body of Christ?" (I Corinthians 10:16 KJV)** Communion was originally two words which were merged to form one—*COMMON* and *UNION*. This translates from the Greek *koinonia*, which is defined as, "the using of a thing in common." We are not brought together by the bread and wine, but by what they symbolically represent—the body and blood of Jesus.

The ceremony we call communion is not an *actual* communion; it is a symbolic testimony that those partaking of it have a *common-union* in Christ. Jesus is our communion; He binds us together. The ceremony simply designates the Purveyor of the bond. As Paul warned the Corinthians:

> For I received from the Lord that which I also delivered to you, that the Lord Jesus in the night in which He was betrayed took bread;

> and when He had given thanks, He broke it, and said, "This is My body, which is for you; do this in REMEMBRANCE of Me."

> In this same way He took the cup also, after supper, saying, "This cup is the new covenant in My blood; do this, as often as you drink it, in REMEMBRANCE of Me."

> For as often as you eat this bread and drink the cup, you proclaim the Lord's death until He comes.

> Therefore whoever eats the bread or drinks the cup of the Lord in an unworthy manner, shall be guilty of the body and the blood of the Lord.

> But let a man examine himself, and so let him eat of the bread and drink of the cup.

> For he who eats and drinks, eats and drinks judgment to himself, if he does not judge the body rightly.

> For this reason many among you are weak and sick, and a number sleep (I Corinthians 11:23-30).

Discerning the Body

If we do not discern the body of Christ rightly, we are pronouncing judgment upon ourselves when we partake of the bread and wine. That is, if we participate in the ritual, assuming it fulfills our obligation to commune with Christ, we have deceived ourselves, and we remain deprived of true Life. The substitution of rituals for realities has repeatedly deprived people of redemption and salvation. **"For this reason many among you are weak and sick, and a number sleep."** If a member of our physical body was cut off from the rest of the body, it would become weak and die very quickly. The same happens when we cut ourselves off from our spiritual body, the church.

As the apostle John declared, **"If we walk in the light as He Himself is in the light, we have fellowship** [Greek *koinonia*: communion] **with one another, and the blood of His Son cleanses us from all sin"** (I John 1:7). The Lord said the life is **"in the blood"** (Leviticus 17:11). If we "commune" with Him, we are joined in one body under the Head so His life's blood can flow through us.

Being properly joined to the body of Christ is not an option if true life is going to flow through us. But let us not substitute being joined to the body with being joined to the Head. By many popular, modern definitions of what it means to be joined to the Lord's body, it has become possible, and even common, to be joined to the body without even having a relationship with the Head.

Much of the church's emphasis over the last half of the twentieth century has been on getting people joined to the body, with very little emphasis on our being joined to the Head. If we are properly joined to the Head, we will be properly joined to the body also, but the reverse is not necessarily true. We must not continue to place the cart in front of the horse in this issue.

Of course, many have used the excuse that they were seeking the Lord in an effort to avoid having a relationship with the church. As Peter related concerning the teachings of Paul: **"in all his letters, speaking in them of these things, in which are some things hard to understand, which the untaught and unstable distort, as they do also the rest of the Scriptures, to their own destruction" (II Peter 3:16).**

There will always be many who distort even the most basic, sound doctrine. Being joined to the Lord and to His body is not an either/or question. We must have both, and we cannot have one without the other. We must esteem our personal relationship with the Lord first, but also be properly related to His body if we are to have life. He said that we must "eat His flesh" *and* "drink His blood."

We Must Eat the Whole Thing

> **Do not eat any of it raw or boiled at all with water, but rather roasted with fire, both its head and its legs along with its entrails.**
>
> **And you shall not leave any of it over until morning... (Exodus 12:9-10).**

Some have become very particular about the gospel, as if it were up to them to choose the aspects of redemption they need. If we are to partake of the Lord's Passover, we must accept every part of Him. He did not give us the option of taking what we want. As He stated in the parable, when we find the pearl of great price, we must buy the whole field in which it was found.

When the Lord commissioned His followers to go and make disciples of all nations, He specifically included **"teaching them to observe ALL that I commanded you" (Matthew 28:20)**. When we come with preconditions of which of His commandments we will accept, we void the very power of the gospel. Often it is that which represents the greatest threat to us that we need the most.

The specific matter that intimidates us is not the important issue; to pick and choose what *we* want is a rejection of His lordship. He cannot be received as Savior unless He also comes as Lord. It is the acceptance of His full lordship which delivers us from the self-centeredness that kills us. Those who claim to have received Him as Savior but continue living according to their own will are deceived. True salvation is the deliverance from self-will and our self-life in exchange for His life. If He is not the Lord *of* all, He is not the Lord *at* all.

When we compromise the gospel to make it acceptable or for any other reason, we strip it of the power to save. Deliverance from the power of evil is not accomplished by merely "turning over a new leaf" and making a few changes in our lives. True deliverance saves us from the "I WILL" so firmly rooted in our fallen nature. It frees us from our futile attempts to build our own towers to heaven.

Satan's original and most successful temptation has been that we could be **"like God"** (see Genesis 3:5). Man's most destructive error is his determination to be his own lord! The whole world esteems and emulates "self-made" men. Yet, if one is self-made, he has actually thwarted his purpose for existence—to *be made* in the image of his Creator. Self-made men are supreme failures. **"What will a man be profited, if he gains the whole world, and forfeits his soul?" (Matthew 16:26)**

The Passover sacrifice of Jesus did not just "paint over" us with His blood, it cleansed us and destroyed the angel of death, the body of sin, and our self-will. Any gospel that preaches salvation without complete surrender is without salvation as well. It is an enemy of the true gospel. A compromised gospel only immunizes us to the truth.

> **"For whoever wishes to save his life shall lose it; but whoever loses his life for My sake shall find it" (Matthew 16:25).**

If we want His life, we must be willing to share His death. When the Lord called a man, he had to leave everything: **"So therefore, no one of you can be My disciple who does not give up all his own possessions" (Luke 14:33).** Whether He requires this of us literally or just in our hearts, it must be real and total. We must all learn the lessons of Job who had to lose everything except the Lord before he knew that the Lord was all he needed. A man who stands in need of nothing but Jesus will not be bound by anything or anyone but Him.

The church today is fragmented. We have assumed the freedom to choose for ourselves which parts of the body of Christ we will accept. We naturally gravitate toward that which is most comfortable. The result has been a debilitating imbalance in most congregations. Those with an evangelistic burden are found in one group, those with a pastoral burden in another, and the prophets in still another. One congregation is all "feet," another "hands," and another "eyes.

These bodies are grotesque substitutes for the perfect body that Christ is determined to have. Each member must be properly joined to the others if the body is to function rightly. Having a perfect heart would be of no benefit without the lungs, kidneys, liver, etc. We presently have all hearts in one place claiming to be the body, all livers in another, and so forth. There must be interchange, interrelationship, and the proper joining of the different parts of the body before there can be an effective functioning of the same.

Pastors have a God-given cautious nature that is protective of the flock. Prophets are visionary by nature, but are also often reckless. Without the balance and influence of the prophetic ministry, pastors will tend to stagnate and become set in their ways. Without the influence of pastors, prophets will drift into extremes, having visions which no one knows how to practically fulfill.

Teachers usually will be very pragmatic in nature, which is essential for clear impartation of the Word. But without prodding from the other ministries, they tend to reduce life in Christ to principles and formulas that are learned by rote.

Evangelists, given to focus on the needs of the lost, often forget to raise and mature them. Yet without evangelists the church will quickly forget the unsaved.

Because apostles are called to be evangelists, prophets, pastors, and teachers, they usually have a more balanced nature and are given for the purpose of keeping the church on the right path.

There Were Two Trees in the Garden

The unity of the Spirit is not a unity by conformity; it is a unity of diversity. For this reason the Lord gave diverse ministries—apostles, prophets, evangelists, pastors, and teachers—to equip the saints (see Ephesians 4:11-12). We must receive *all* the ministries. To partake of the Lord's body, we must "eat the whole thing."

We are exhorted to **"grow up in *all* aspects into Him, who is the head" (Ephesians 4:15).** The apostles were directed to **"speak to the people in the temple the whole message of this Life" (Acts 5:20).** The psalmist discerned that **"the SUM of Thy word is truth" (Psalm 119:160).** We can be distracted from the Truth by individual truths. We can be distracted from the River of Life by the individual tributaries which feed it.

Almost all denominations are built around a single emphasis. They may teach other aspects, but emphasize one small portion of the whole revelation of God. Any time we focus our attention on one part of the whole, our scope will be limited. Only when we focus on the Truth (Jesus) do all truths take their proper perspective. Jesus is the sum of God's Word.

Until we see Jesus as the summation of all spiritual truth, we are like the proverbial blind men trying to comprehend the elephant—one thought it was a tree because he had found its leg; another thought it was a fan because he had found an ear; another thought it was a whip because he had found the tail, and so it goes. They were all correct, yet each would be deceived about the true nature of the elephant until they perceived the whole.

Individual aspects of God's Word may be interpreted falsely apart from the whole Word. The Lord emphasized the fact that the Scriptures have eternal life in them only if they testify of Him (see John 5:39-40). Overemphasis in one area is indicative of partial, incomplete comprehension of the whole. As Paul explained to the Hebrews, **"God, after He spoke long ago to the fathers in the prophets in many portions and in many ways, in these last days has spoken to us in His Son" (Hebrews 1:1-2).** The Father is no longer giving us fragments. He has given us the whole Loaf.

We may have such a vision of the united and perfected body of Christ that we are sure this church will draw all men to itself. However, the church is not to draw men to itself, but rather is commissioned to equip those whom the Lord has drawn. It is only when Jesus is lifted up that men will be drawn together, and they will be drawn to HIM! King David perceived this and wrote the "Psalm of Unity:" **"Behold, how good and how pleasant it is for brothers to dwell together in unity! It is like the precious oil UPON THE HEAD [Jesus], coming down upon the beard...coming down upon the edge of his robes" (Psalm 133:1-2).**

If we anoint the Head with our worship and devotion, the oil will run down and cover the whole body (of Christ). There will one day be a church that is perfected in unity, but it is likely that she will not even be aware of how glorious she is. Her attention will be on Jesus, not herself.

Chapter 16
THE SPIRIT IS MOVING

Now you shall eat it in this manner: with your loins girded, your sandals on your feet, and your staff in your hand; and you shall eat it in HASTE (Exodus 12:11).

INCLUDED IN THE PASSOVER WAS THE FEAST OF UNLEAVENED Bread (see Exodus 12:14-20). For seven days, beginning with the first day of the Passover, Israel could not eat any leavened bread. This was meant to remind the Israelites of their flight from Egypt, when they left in such haste that their bread did not have time to become leavened:

And they baked the dough which they had brought out of Egypt into cakes of unleavened bread. For it had not become leavened, since they were driven out of Egypt and could not delay... (Exodus 12:39).

Because of its permeating characteristics, leaven (yeast) is symbolic of sin in Scripture:

...Do you not know that a little leaven leavens the whole lump of dough?

Clean out the old leaven, that you may be a new lump, just as you are in fact unleavened. For Christ our Passover also has been sacrificed.

Let us therefore celebrate the feast, not with old leaven, nor with the leaven of malice and wickedness, but with the unleavened bread of sincerity and truth (I Corinthians 5:6-8).

Leaven is also symbolic of doctrine that is legalistic in nature. The Lord warned His disciples to **"beware of the leaven of the Pharisees and Sadducees" (Matthew 16:6)**. Not long after the gospel began to spread, converts from the Pharisees tried to bring the young church under the yoke of the Law. Satan was trying to seduce the young bride of Christ with the same deception used to seduce the bride of the first Adam—to eat of the Tree of the Knowledge of Good and Evil. After great controversy, the apostles and elders sent word to all of the churches in what was a most important and historic communiqué:

For it seemed good to the Holy Spirit and to us to lay upon you no greater burden than these essentials:

that you abstain from things sacrificed to idols and from blood and from things strangled and from fornication; if you keep yourselves free from such things, you will do well (Acts 15:28-29).

Webster's New World Dictionary defines leaven as "a substance such as yeast used to produce fermentation, especially in dough." The same dictionary defines fermentation as "a state of excitement; agitation; commotion; unrest." The apostles and elders in Jerusalem noted that the Pharisee converts produced the same characteristics in the church: **"since we have heard that some of our number to whom we gave no instruction have *disturbed* you with their words, unsettling your souls" (Acts 15:24).** Such are the characteristics of spiritual leaven.

Doctrines that disturb and unsettle the body of Christ are often rooted in legalism. There is a continual pressure upon the church to walk in principles and/or formulas to gain maturity. These doctrines usually seem **"good for food...a delight to the eyes, and...desirable to make one wise" (Genesis 3:6).** Satan could not tempt us if the fruit were not appealing. Laws, principles, and formulas are appealing because they offer the security of a known commodity. Walking by law or principles gives us the control that our insecurity demands. But this is a false security. It is security in ourselves rather than in the One who alone offers true security.

A Righteousness Greater Than the Law

"For all who are being led by the Spirit of God, these are sons of God" (Romans 8:14). As discussed earlier, walking by the Spirit does not mean that we do not keep the Law. If we walk by the Spirit, we do *more* than keep the Law—we fulfill it! For example, the Law says we are not to covet our neighbor's wife or property. The Spirit calls us to an even higher way, to *love* our neighbor. If we love our neighbor, of course we will not covet what is his, nor in any way do him harm.

The Spirit does not just command love, but He imparts the *ability* to love—with His love. Jesus did not come to destroy the Law, but to fulfill it. He came to lift us *above* the Law, giving us the power to exceed its requirements.

Walking in the Spirit is life, peace, and fulfillment, but it is difficult. It is difficult because the flesh wars against the Spirit. The "I WILL" nature of Cain within us will not easily submit to the Spirit. There is a determination in the flesh to "be as God" and to rule its own destiny. This determination to control desperately resists relinquishing control. But if we are to live by the Spirit, Jesus alone must be our Master.

It is easier to make rules than to be sensitive to the Spirit. Regulations can bring order and relieve many pressures, but they cannot change the inner man. A time is coming when the regulations will not be able to cope with the chaos. We must have a more solid foundation. If we are seeking order and security in our religion, we will lose both.

The fear of deception will not keep us from deception; it will lead into it. We must not walk by fear but by faith. The Scripture testifies that the only thing that will keep us from deception is to have a *love for the Truth*, (see II Thessalonians 2:10), Jesus. When we open our shades at night, darkness does not come in, but rather light shines out into the darkness. Light overcomes darkness because it is more powerful.

If we seek to do our Father's will and serve Him, we will find an order and security that no degree of chaos can overcome. We must be able to hear and distinguish His voice from all the other voices in the world. When the shaking comes—and it will (see Hebrews 12:25-29)—knowing His voice and following Him will be the only true security we have.

Does this mean that we should do away with all laws, rules, and regulations in society? Certainly not! As the apostle explained: **"But we know that the Law is good, if one uses it lawfully, realizing the fact that law is not made for a righteous man** [those in Christ], **but for those who are lawless and rebellious, for the ungodly and sinners, for the unholy and profane..." (I Timothy 1:8-9).** In the world, laws and regulations are necessary to maintain a semblance of order until the kingdom comes, but it is futile to use them to impose spiritual discipline—only the Spirit can beget that which is spirit.

The Bible is God's instruction book for human beings. It contains the greatest wisdom ever written. It gives important instructions about how humans really work, accurately describing both our potential and what causes our problems. Yet as marvelous as this gift is, the Bible was given to lead us *to* Jesus, *not* to take His place.

Spiritual Order

The Scriptures say amazingly little concerning the government of the church. That is why it is essential for His sheep to know His voice. The church must be ruled and guided by the Head rather than by formulas or organizational structures. The church is first and foremost a family, not an institution. When we stop being a family and start becoming an organization, we cease to be the church.

Families are governed by relationships, not just decrees. The Lord is purposely vague concerning even important issues so that we have to seek Him. The New Testament is full of the best counsel the world has ever heard, but the Lord and His apostles were careful not to lay down many general rules and regulations for the churches. They knew that every rule could inadvertently prevent the believers from seeking the Lord for themselves.

Developing a vital relationship with Him is the important work the Spirit is doing in us. The Spirit was sent to lead us to Jesus. Used as a rule book, the Bible becomes the letter that kills, the Tree of Knowledge, and can even become an idol. Used properly, it turns us to Him and helps us walk with Him, abide in Him, and know Him—not just know about Him.

The Pharisees confronted every problem with a new rule. The Lord referred to their doctrines as leaven, because they caused agitation and commotion among the people. When we try to confront problems in the church with new regulations, we are sowing leaven. Like the doctrines of the Pharisees, these only clean up the outside; they are not able to deal with the true problem. They may bring a degree of control and order, but the greatest order found among people is in the cemetery!

When order takes the place of having a relationship with the Lord, that is usually what we end up with—a spiritual cemetery. The dead do not cause problems! The spiritually dead will have an orderly church. But the Lord came to give *abundant* life (see John 10:10). Abundance does not dictate that it be all good; it just means there is a lot of it! It includes the good and the bad.

Living by regulations will give outward order, but it will breed inner agitation and unrest. There is no true rest in the law until there is death—making men machines or zombies instead of humans who are able to have a relationship with their Creator. Jesus is **"the Lord of the Sabbath,"** **(Matthew 12:8)**, or the Lord of rest. Abiding in Him we have life and peace. He says to us, **"Cease striving and know that I AM God" (Psalm 46:10).** The Law makes us look at ourselves, where we will only see death and corruption. The Spirit shows us Jesus and creates a yearning that keeps us always in pursuit of Him.

"The unfolding of Thy words gives light" says the psalmist (Psalm 119:130). There is unfathomable depth of revelation we have not yet realized in God's Word, even concerning the most basic doctrines. It is a terrible mistake to become satisfied with our present level of knowledge and understanding. We are all seeing through a glass darkly. We cannot know anything fully until we know Him fully. **"But the path of the righteous is like the light of dawn, that shines brighter and brighter until the full day" (Proverbs 4:18).** When the truth stops expanding for us, we begin to live in darkness.

Water is often used symbolically as the Word of God in Scripture (see Ephesians 5:26). When the Lord uses a natural type to symbolize a spiritual reality, it is because its characteristics reflect the nature of the spiritual. One important characteristic of water is that it must keep flowing in order to stay pure. Once it settles in one place, it becomes stagnant very quickly—and so does the Word of God. Every revelation of truth in our lives should be continually expanding and deepening for us. That is why the River of Life is just that—a river! It is not a pond or a lake—it is flowing, moving, and going somewhere. As an old sage once remarked, "You can never step into the same river twice."

Having truth that expands is threatening to those who are of the spirit of the Pharisees. Although they have a zeal for the Lord and a desire for purity of truth, their real security is in the human traditions with which they insulate the truth. With those who are of this spirit, there will be a de facto elevating of orthodoxy to the same level as biblical revelation, even though they would vehemently deny that this is so. When we hunger for deeper understanding and insight, the potential for erroneous revelation does exist. But if we do *not* seek deeper revelation, we already have made a fatal and debilitating error. *Having truth will not keep us from deception, but having a love for the truth will.*

We Must Eat in Haste

Israel's bread did not have time to become leavened because Egypt was left in such haste. In the same way, if we will keep moving on with the Spirit, our "bread" will not have time to become leavened with sin, wickedness, or legalism. It is when we stop moving and growing that our "bread" becomes infected.

We have discussed how the Passover lamb was taken into the houses of Israel to be thoroughly examined for five days before the sacrifice, and how this may reflect the need to thoroughly examine Christ before making a commitment. Yet we see here that once the commitment is made, we must then move in haste to flee the land of Egypt.

It is interesting to note the *immediacy* with which a new believer was baptized in the early church. This shows that after a true commitment is made, it needs to be sealed at once with the biblical ordinance given for the public demonstration of faith, which is water baptism. Nowhere in Scripture do we find such things as an altar call, the raising of hands, or the myriad of other customs we have substituted for the biblical rite of immediate baptism. These human devices, which have been instituted mostly for the sake of convenience, have often proven counter-productive in sealing the commitment of the new believer.

How much more impact would the "decision" have on new converts if we faithfully complied with the biblical mandate for immediate baptism? How much more would their commitment stand as a powerful signpost in their lives if they could see a biblical testimony of their action, in place of the vague wonder-if-anything-really-happened walk down an aisle or brief raising of their hands?

Chapter 17
NO STRANGERS MAY EAT OF IT

This is the ordinance of the Passover: no foreigner [stranger] **is to eat of it (Exodus 12:43).**

A S THE CHURCH GROWS IN THE GRACE AND KNOWLEDGE OF our Lord, we will become more tolerant, but this does not mean we will be all-inclusive. History testifies that each restoration of truth to the church is vulnerable to getting diluted or stamped out by the sheer multitudes who embrace it. Our tendency to seek security through the approval of numbers has cost the church immeasurably by watering down the power of the pure and uncompromised truth. We are warned to beware when all men think well of us. Did people not heartily hail the false prophets? (see Luke 6:26) We must be secure only in our justification and approval from God. **"The fear of man brings a snare" (Proverbs 29:25).**

A door has two functions: to let people in and to keep them out. Jesus is the Door. When we allow those to join the church who have not come through the Door, we place both the congregation and the unconverted in jeopardy. This is not to say that unsaved people should be excluded from our services, but they should not be included as members of the body of Christ until they have been joined to the Head.

Vain Worship

New buildings, family life centers, projects, and programs have drawn many into the churches. They may have also helped to keep some in churches. But they have never drawn a man to Christ. We may even think that the dynamic spirituality of our fellowship will bring men to Him, but it never will. The church can actually be a distraction and hindrance to true conversion if it allows membership in the church without rebirth in Jesus. Mere church attendance and activism can actually work against the conviction the Holy Spirit is seeking to bring into our lives, for it may enable us to feel safe in a spiritual condition in which we remain lost.

One of the first things God said was *not good* was for man to be alone. He made us social creatures and therefore we all crave strong social ties. The true church is the most dynamic social entity the world has ever known. We must be careful that people are not drawn to our assemblies instead of to the Lord. It is common for people to say the right things, change their outward behavior, and even sincerely believe the doctrine of Christ in their minds without knowing Jesus in their hearts. It is possible to be quite "spiritual" and yet not know Him, as the Lord Himself warned:

"Many will say to Me on that day, 'Lord, Lord, did we not prophesy in Your name, and in Your name cast out demons, and in Your name perform many miracles?'

"And then I will declare to them, 'I never knew you; depart from Me, you who practice lawlessness'" (Matthew 7:22-23).

"As the branch cannot bear fruit of itself, unless it abides in the vine, so neither can you, unless you abide in Me" (John 15:4).

To be joined to the church through Christ is life and power, but seeking union with Christ through the church is vain. We have often made it easy for one to be attached to the body without being joined to the Head. One cannot be joined to Christ without being joined to His body. Paul scrupulously presented Christ crucified to the unsaved. He understood that if people were drawn by anything but Jesus, the conversion could be false. Paul's confidence was not in psychology or methodology. He used something much more powerful—THE GOSPEL.

There is great danger in "not discerning the body rightly" and allowing those to join with us who have not come through the Door. It is also dangerous to presume knowledge of another's spiritual condition or his standing before God when it is not *obvious*. There are certain basic truths we must agree upon in order to walk together, essentially the atonement and lordship of Jesus. However, when we become exclusive based on doctrines which go beyond the revelation of Jesus as the Door, we are in danger of cutting ourselves off from the body of Christ and becoming a sect or even a cult.

The Habitation of God

The Tabernacle of Moses was a type of both the Lord Jesus and the church, as both were to be the habitation of God. In Moses' Tabernacle, the closer one came to the presence of the Lord, the more sanctified he was required to be. Our situation is similar. The apostle exhorts, **"Pursue peace with all men** [tolerance]**, and the sanctification** [separation] **without which no one will see the Lord" (Hebrews 12:14).**

When the Tabernacle of Moses was constructed and consecrated for use, an unsanctified man could not enter the Holy Place or even look upon the furniture inside. The penalty for this was death (see Numbers 4:20). This was to testify of the requirement of sanctification before we can see the most holy things. When a man living in darkness is suddenly exposed to great light, he will not be enlightened; he will be blinded! Because of this, we must be discerning when exposing unbelievers, or new believers, to the deeper truths of the Lord. Meat will not nourish babies; it will choke them.

Because acacia wood was twisted, knotty, and hard to work with, it is often typical of fallen human nature in Scripture. In the outer court of the Tabernacle of Moses, the furniture was made of acacia wood overlaid with bronze and was illumined by the natural light of the sun. This testified of the fact that men who just enter the outer court usually only have their sinful nature "covered" and walk more by the "natural" light.

When we enter the Tabernacle, we come into the compartment called the Holy Place. The furniture here was also made of acacia wood, but was covered with pure gold. Gold, being incorruptible, is symbolic of the divine nature. The only light in the Holy Place was provided by olive oil burned in a lampstand, the olive oil being symbolic of the anointing of the Holy Spirit.

In the Holy Place, there is no natural light. We cannot function there with our natural minds, but are utterly dependent on the Holy Spirit. In the Holy of Holies, the innermost compartment where the Lord Himself dwells, the Ark of the Covenant was made of acacia wood covered with gold inside and out. The light provided in the Holy of Holies is the very presence of the Lord. We see by this that the closer one gets to the glory of the Lord, the more gold there is. This illustrates that we are changed into the divine nature by the glory (see II Corinthians 3:18). As we come closer to the glory, the light by which we walk changes from natural light to the anointing of the Holy Spirit, and then to the very presence and glory of the Lord.

"Our God is a consuming fire" (Hebrews 12:29). Had the acacia wood been exposed to the fire of God's glory without being covered by the gold, it would have been consumed. For our sakes, sanctification is required to see the Lord and to draw close to Him, lest we be consumed (see Hebrews 12:14).

Unfortunately, many have a concept of the Father as being the angry God of the Old Testament, who would destroy us if Jesus did not mediate and assuage His wrath. We must not forget that it was the Father who sent His Son because He **"so loved the world" (John 3:16).** The Father Himself loves us, and He desires fellowship with us so much that He subjected His own Son to torture and death in order that we might draw near to Him. Even so,

God is holy, and His holiness is a consuming fire. That is why sanctification is required to see Him. If we are still wood, hay, and stubble, we will be consumed by His presence (see I Corinthians 3:11-15).

It is only as we have come to more fully abide in His Son, being covered by more and more of the gold of His divine nature, that we are able to draw closer and closer to the Father. It was the crucifixion of Jesus that rent the veil which separated us from the Father. It is as we are "crucified with Christ," and His cleansing blood is applied to our lives, that the way is made for us to boldly enter into the Father's presence, which is His heart's desire.

The ministry in the Outer Court is to the people. The ministry in the Holy Place and Holy of Holies is to the Lord. This is what transforms us. Without this ministry to the Lord, we will not be as effective in our Outer Court ministry. We must carry light from the Lord, but we cannot take the people into that light until they have been sanctified. No strangers may partake of the Passover of the Lord, and those who have not discerned the body rightly should not partake of the bread and wine of the Lord's Supper.

The Three Levels of Ministry

Just as there were three dimensions to the tabernacle ministry, the ministry of Jesus had three basic levels: to the multitude, the twelve, and then the three. He spoke to the multitudes in parables and basics (the Outer Court). To the twelve He revealed the mysteries, and they experienced the anointing (the Holy Place). Only the three—Peter, James, and John—were privileged to see His glory on the Mount of Transfiguration (the Holy of Holies).

Pastors who are evangelical in orientation will have congregations which focus mostly on the Outer Court aspect of the ministry. Pastors gifted in teaching will tend to have congregations which emphasize ministry typified by the Holy Place. Churches led by prophets will seek to abide in the Holy of Holies. Properly balanced congregations, however, will have a ministry on all three levels, as the Lord and the tabernacle exemplify.

Every congregation and minister needs to have an outreach to the lost and a ministry to Christians at all levels of maturity. Failure to do so leads to imbalance and often error. If we do not have new converts, there will be stagnation. If we do not have meetings devoted entirely to worshiping the Lord without the distraction of human pressure, demands, and even needs, there will be superficiality and a lack of anointing and power for the ministry to the people.

Recognizing the importance of providing ministry for all levels of maturity is essential, but we must understand that it is wrong to distinguish and value people according to their level of maturity. The purpose for each level of ministry is to prepare people for the next higher level. If the ministry is functioning properly, everyone will be maturing and entering higher levels of experience, effectiveness, and intimacy with the Lord Himself. Those in ministry need to discern a person's maturity level in order to serve him effectively, not to label him as a certain class of Christian.

Some have taken this understanding of the levels of maturity to classify and distinguish themselves as superior or others as inferior. This will inevitably happen. As Peter remarked concerning Paul's teachings, there were some things in them that were hard to understand, which the unstable and untaught distorted, just as they did the rest of the Scriptures (see II Peter 3:15-16). Pride in a man's heart will cause him to use even the Scriptures to feed his ego. One of true humility will only be further humbled by the greatest accolades of God and man.

True humility is not an inferiority complex. True humility comes from seeing the majesty of the Lord. As the apostle explained, those who measure themselves by themselves (or with each other) were without understanding (see II Corinthians 10:12). In God's kingdom, authority and position exist for serving. The faithful and obedient ministry of helps is more esteemed by God than the most noteworthy apostle who considers himself higher than others.

The Reason for the Tares

There will be tares growing among the wheat in the church. Even the apostle Paul ordained elders who would prove to be wolves (see Acts 20:29-30). Jesus chose Judas and included him in the inner circle. Though the tares among us may cause great damage and confusion, they are actually working out the purposes of God. All things work for the good of those who love God (see Romans 8:28). Such disruptions almost always result in our becoming more dependent on the Lord and less dependent on those who are but flesh and blood.

This is not to say that we should purposely ordain traitors and include false brethren in our assemblies! But we can be sure it will happen and that it will nevertheless work out for our good.

During the 1960s and 70s, there was a major emphasis on "submission" in the body of Christ. This was a word from God, and only He knows how badly we needed it because of the rebellion then surfacing in the world. But we quickly formed our doctrines on submission and started judging men by how well they conformed to the doctrine, instead of looking for the fruit of submission in their lives. As a result of this, many unbroken and rebellious ministries were released upon the church by virtue of their outward conformance to the doctrine of submission. Likewise, some truly broken and submissive men and women of God were almost blackballed from ministry because they did not conform to the doctrine. The devastation caused by this shallowness is now history.

In the coming years, humility will become an emphasis. This is a timely and important word, but let us not make the same mistake with it as we did with submission. The Lord does resist the proud and give grace to the humble (see James 4:6), but it is so much better when we let Him do it. We must begin to know one another after the Spirit and not after the flesh.

Only the Spirit can judge accurately. Appearances are almost always deceiving. King Saul appeared humble; it was said that he was small in his own eyes (see I Samuel 15:17 NIV). David appeared arrogant and insolent, rebuking the armies of Israel for their timidity and saying that the king's own armor was not good enough for him. We must rise above the tendency to follow the first one who appears to be head and shoulders above the rest.

There Were Two Trees in the Garden

Those whom we judge as tares by our own understanding may well be wheat and vice versa. That is why the Lord instructed us to let the wheat and tares grow together until the harvest. Until there is maturity, the wheat and tares may look so much alike that it will be almost impossible to tell them apart. Both may be arrogant; they may both even have false concepts or teaching or fall into sin occasionally. The difference will only be obvious when they both mature. During the harvest, wheat will bow over, while the tares remain standing upright. When wheat matures it becomes humble, but those who are in fact tares will continue in their pride.

Let us also not forget God's grace or His judgment. Some who are tares may repent and become wheat. Likewise, some who are wheat will fall and become stumbling blocks in our midst. That "no strangers are to partake of the Passover" (see Exodus 12:43) is a truth, but let us be careful how we apply it. Those who have not entered through the Door are obvious. Judging beyond that is difficult and dangerous, and can lead to grievous errors.

If we are walking in the light, we will allow truth to remain at the point of divine tension between the extremes and will refrain from making a formula, principle, or inflexible doctrine out of it. It is the fruit of the Tree of Knowledge which demands our carrying the paradoxes in Scripture to their logical conclusions. The paradoxes are there to force us to seek the Lord for His mind and wisdom. This leads to our walking by the Spirit instead of by principles or laws. By resisting the compulsion to make formulas and by allowing truth to rest at the point of tension between the extremes, we begin to partake of the Tree of Life. Christianity is not just following a set of rules; it is walking with God.

Chapter 18
THE VICTORY

Now the sons of Israel had done according to the word of Moses, for they had requested from the Egyptians articles of silver and articles of gold, and clothing;

and the LORD had given the people favor in the sight of the Egyptians, so that they let them have their request. Thus they plundered the Egyptians (Exodus 12:35-36).

AFTER BEING SLAVES FOR FOUR HUNDRED YEARS, ISRAEL partook of the Passover and became wealthier than in their wildest imagination. When we partake of the true Passover which is Christ, in Him we are given the right to become the sons of God—joint heirs of the world and all it contains. Even so, all of the world's riches are as nothing compared to the spiritual riches which are in Christ. But just as it is written, **"Things which eye has not seen and ear has not heard, and which have not entered the heart of man, all that God has prepared for** those who love Him" (**I Corinthians 2:9**). Truly, in Christ we have inherited more riches than we are capable of imagining.

Israel left Egypt weighted down with wealth, but their bounty was not taken to the closest bazaar so they could spend it. God took them into the wilderness where they could not spend even a single shekel! There they were able to invest their riches toward something more valuable than anything the world could sell them—the tabernacle, a habitation for God so He might dwell among them.

Today the body of Christ receives a great deal of teaching about the riches we have in Christ. This teaching is timely. For centuries the church has been deprived of the inheritance she has in Christ. Sadly, this emphasis has often been devoted more to the material than the eternal. This is the delusion of slaves who one day dramatically find themselves kings. We have been removed from Egypt, but in many ways Egypt has not yet been removed from us. However, it is encouraging that many are beginning to reject this mentality and envision the incomparable riches of Christ.

> **Blessed be the God and Father of our Lord Jesus Christ, who has blessed us with every *spiritual blessing* in the *heavenly places* in Christ (Ephesians 1:3).**

When we perceive our *spiritual* blessings in Christ, *material* blessings lose their appeal. If someone were to discover a vein of gold that could provide the entire world's needs forever, would he continue panning for mere nuggets? We have that vein in the person of our Lord Jesus. Why do we give so much attention to the things which pass away? It is because we have not truly seen Him as He is; we have merely discovered a few things about Him.

In Hebrews 11 (popularly referred to as "the faith chapter"), there is a long list of the great triumphs of faith. These are wonderful testimonies of God's faithfulness to those who call upon Him in faith. Many deliverances are taking place today that are just as wonderful. But seldom is the last part of that chapter noted:

>...and others were tortured, *not accepting their release, in order that they might obtain a better resurrection;*

>and others experienced mockings and scourgings, yes, also chains and imprisonment.

>They were stoned, they were sawn in two, they were tempted, they were put to death with the sword;

>they went about in sheepskins, in goatskins, *being destitute*, afflicted, ill-treated (men of whom the world was not worthy), wandering in deserts and mountains and caves and holes in the ground.

>And all these, having gained approval through their faith, did not receive what was promised,

>because God had provided something better for us, so that apart from us they should not be made perfect (Hebrews 11:35-40).

These who were seeking a **"better resurrection"** did not quench the power of fire or close the mouths of lions—they would not even accept their release! They did not live in palaces; they lived in holes in the ground and in caves. The Lord Jesus Himself did not even have a place to lay His head (see Matthew 8:20). When we begin to see the spiritual riches in Christ, it will not matter to us where we live.

If Jesus is in it, a cave will have more glory than the greatest human structure. To live in a cave or palace will make little difference if we abide in Him. Some think it is more spiritual to be abased and others that it is more spiritual to abound, but neither is true. We may be in error if we are trying to live an abased life that God has not called us to, or vice versa. The issue is being in the will of the Lord and keeping a steadfast devotion to Him whether we are abounding or being abased.

Cain was the father of those who are earthly minded; he was a **"tiller of the ground" (Genesis 4:2)**. Those who are still carnal will always be seekers of earthly gain, regardless of the spiritual guise. The kingdom of our Lord and His chosen is not of this world. Those who seek His kingdom are strangers and sojourners. Here they have no lasting city, and they are not trying to build one, for they are seeking the city whose architect and builder is God.

We cannot attain this heart of the spiritual sojourner by seeking it. Those who seek to be unearthly for its own sake, believing it to be spiritual, usually become sad examples of spiritual barrenness. **"For as many as may be the promises of God, in Him they are yes" (II Corinthians 1:20)**. The promises of God are positives, not negatives. A failure to understand this is why some of the most worldly and unspiritual men are found in monasteries and secluded spiritual communities. (This is not to imply that all who are found in these are so.)

The truly spiritual man is thus because his heart is so captured by the things of the Spirit that he simply has no time or interest for the things of the world. Once we have beheld the spiritual riches that are found in Christ, going back to worldly interests could be compared to a billionaire sweeping streets for minimum wages. Those who still have a love for worldly pleasures simply have not received the love of the Father (see I John 2:15). As Paul explained to the Colossians:

> **If you have died with Christ to the elementary principles of the world, why, as if you were living in the world, do you submit yourself to decrees, such as,**

> **"Do not handle, do not taste, do not touch!"**

> **(which all refer to things destined to perish with the using)—in accordance with the commandments and teachings of men?**

> **These are matters which have, to be sure, the appearance of wisdom in self-made religion and self-abasement and severe treatment of the body, *but are of no value against fleshly indulgence* (Colossians 2:20-23).**

True spirituality is not just a distaste for the world and its interests; it is a consuming love for the things of the Spirit and the interests of our God. This can only come when the eyes of our hearts have been opened so that the things of the Spirit are more real to us than the things which are seen with the eyes of our minds.

The Waving of the Sheaf

As a fitting last touch to this remarkable Feast of the Passover, the Lord instituted what is called "The Waving of the Sheaf of the Firstfruits" (see Leviticus 23:9-15). This feast was celebrated in early spring as the first shoots of the coming harvest were just sprouting. On the morning after the Passover Sabbath, a sheaf of this first evidence of the coming harvest was brought to the priest and he waved it before the Lord. As this ritual was being performed after the Passover of our Lord's crucifixion, Jesus was bursting forth from His tomb!

Jesus was the Sheaf of the firstfruits of the resurrection, who at that very time was being waved before the Father as evidence of the coming great harvest, perfectly fulfilling the type.

It is an interesting fact that more Scripture is devoted to Abraham's choosing of a burial place for his family than to such important subjects as being born again or church order. Isaac and Jacob insisted on being buried there, and Joseph made the sons of Israel swear to carry his bones up from Egypt to bury him there. It is a great enigma as to why the patriarchs gave so much importance to where they were to be buried, until we read Matthew 27:50-53:

> **And Jesus cried out again with a loud voice, and yielded up His spirit.**
>
> **And behold, the veil of the temple was torn in two from top to bottom, and the earth shook; and the rocks were split,**
>
> **and the tombs were opened; and many bodies of the saints who had fallen asleep were raised;**

and coming out of the tombs *after His resurrection* they entered the holy city and appeared to many.

The burial ground which Abraham had chosen for his family was just outside of Jerusalem. As the Lord Himself confirmed, Abraham was a prophet who had foreseen His resurrection: **"Your father Abraham rejoiced to see My day, and he saw it and was glad"** (John 8:56). Abraham and those of his family who had vision made a provision to be a part of the first resurrection.

The patriarchs were not just concerned about where they were buried but where they would be raised. Those who have vision are also making provision by how they are buried as to how they will be raised. If we have been buried with Christ, we shall also be raised with Him (see Romans 6:5). Every Christian is called to be a martyr— every day! We make provision for our resurrection every day, by laying down our lives and being buried with Him. In this light, one of the greatest men of vision of all time gave the church what may be his most important exhortation:

> **For we are the true circumcision, who worship in the Spirit of God and glory in Christ Jesus and put no confidence in the flesh (Philippians 3:3).**

> **More than that, I count all things to be loss in view of the surpassing value of knowing Christ Jesus my Lord, for whom I have suffered the loss of all things, and count them but rubbish in order that I may gain Christ,**

and may be found in Him, not having a righteousness of my own derived from the Law, but that which is through faith in Christ, the righteousness which comes from God on the basis of faith,

that I may know Him, and the power of His resurrection and the fellowship of His sufferings, being conformed to His death;

in order that I may attain to the resurrection from the dead.

Not that I have already obtained it, or have already become perfect, but I press on in order that I may lay hold of that for which also I was laid hold of by Christ Jesus.

Brethren, I do not regard myself as having laid hold of it yet; but one thing I do: forgetting what lies behind and reaching forward to what lies ahead,

I press on toward the goal for the prize of the upward call of God in Christ Jesus (Philippians 3:8-14).

Paul's declaration, **"one thing I do,"** reflects the singleness of his mind on this issue. When our eye or vision is likewise single, our whole body will be full of light. Only then will we know true resurrection life and power.